SHATTERING THE MYTH

Signposts on Custer's Road to Disaster

KEVIN M. SULLIVAN

Copyright © 1995, Kevin M. Sullivan
All Rights Reserved

No part of this book may be reproduced or transmitted in any form or by any means, electronic, mechanical, including photocopying, recording, or by any information storage and retrieval system, except in the case of reviews, without the express written permission of the publisher, except where permitted by law.

Library of Congress Catalog Number 95-70981
ISBN Number 1-57087-195-7

Professional Press
Chapel Hill, North Carolina 27515-4371

Manufactured in the United States of America
96 95 94 93 92   10 9 8 7 6 5 4 3 2 1

The cover photograph was taken in April, 1876

For Sarah, who truly is the light of my life.

Contents

Preface	I
Chapter One: *True Heart of the Warrior*	1
Chapter Two: *When Worlds Collide*	17
Chapter Three: *The Year of Premonitions*	37
Chapter Four: *Valley of Fear*	51
Chapter Five: *Field of Death*	71
Chapter Six: *Alive, and on the Hill*	85
Conclusion	101
Acknowledgments	111
Notes	113
Bibliography	119
Author	122

PREFACE

Much has changed in the world since that day in June 1876, when George Armstrong Custer and five companies of his Seventh Cavalry perished under a broiling Montana sun. Many conflicts, great and small, have occurred over the last one hundred and nineteen years, filling the history books with the names of winners and losers from around the globe. Yet for many Americans, the Battle of Little Bighorn has continued to hold a unique place within the American psyche despite this passage of time. One can study bloodier battles, engaging larger armies, and lasting far longer than that which occurred between the United States military and the native Americans on that day. Yet this battle is unique for a number of reasons, all of which would continue to produce changes for both cultures long after the smoke of battle had drifted away from the field.

First, the Indians were under no illusions concerning their final outcome in the summer of 1876. Yet they were like anyone else who cherishes freedom and has no desire to go

Shattering the Myth

gently into that good night. And so, when Custer came looking for battle, they did not disappoint him. And while the defeat of Custer must be considered their greatest victory against the whites, it would be bittersweet, for it would signal quite clearly the beginning of the end of their way of life. After Little Bighorn, a new, determined sense of wrath was kindled among those seeking an end to what they considered a long overdue problem. Even so, this battle would prove to be pivotal for the whites as well.

In one fell swoop the Sioux and Cheyenne warriors shattered the myth of Custer as the unconquerable warrior. The death of George Armstrong Custer ended the life of one of the most flamboyant, brave, careless, and fascinating characters to ever wear a United States military uniform. His dramatic rise during the Civil War to the brevet (or temporary) rank of brigadier general at the tender age of twenty-three, and his uncanny ability to stay alive regardless of how recklessly he flung himself at the enemy, gave rise to his image as an almost mythical figure. Even President Abraham Lincoln heard about this dashing young warrior whose name had become a household word. General Sheridan was so pleased with him that, after General Grant and General Lee signed the formal papers of surrender at Appomattox, Sheridan purchased the table upon which the documents had been signed, and gave it to Custer as a gift for his wife. Forever after, Custer would be seen as the darling of the nation. More than anything else, he would be remembered by his generation as the boy-general who went from victory to victory, whose life was filled with such good fortune that the term "Custer's luck" was used to refer to an unusually fortuitous incident.

Yet if Custer could rise today from his tomb at West Point, he would be horrified to know that his fame, only one century later, would spring from this very quick battle which resulted not only in his death, but in one of the worst military defeats in U.S. history. Not a great legacy, to be sure, but history never promises to be kind in remembering us, only to remember.

But what really happened at Little Bighorn, and what thoughts were flowing through the mind of Custer on that fateful day? To what degree Custer was at fault is debated among students of the battle to this very day. To Custer, the idea of his beloved Seventh Cavalry ever being defeated by an untrained, undisciplined, and unorganized group of plains Indians never entered his mind. Such arrogant heads had been raised in the U.S. military before, only to be lopped off by untrained, undisciplined, and unorganized—but very determined—warriors.

When, on June 25, the scout Bloody Knife warned him that there were more Sioux awaiting them than they had bullets, he merely responded, "Well, I guess we'll get through them in one day." But instead of getting through them in one day, this myth would evaporate before the eyes of Custer in little more time than it takes to consume a meal, according to one Indian participant.

Yet his miscalculation of the unstoppable power of his regiment would not be the only miscalculation of the campaign. Indeed, it would prove to be only one of many. His refusal to heed the advice of his scouts as to the size of the village they were attacking would also add to their undoing. His belief that the Indians would flee at the first sign of trouble also proved false, but by the time Custer realized his mistake his fate was irretrievably sealed. Tragically, his decision to split the regiment guaranteed disaster. Once the command was separated, Custer and his five companies were quickly drawn into the vortex from which there would be no escape.

In light of this, I believe it is fair to say that Custer died not so much from Sioux and Cheyenne bullets, as from wrong thinking. As was always the case when it came to leading men into battle, Custer was going to do things his way. What is so ironic is that in Custer, the Indians had an ally, and soon many lives would be sacrificed on the altar of his ignorance. That the command would escape complete annihilation, given the perilous position in which Custer had placed them, is all the more surprising.

But to understand Custer the Indian fighter, one must understand the Custer who came charging out of the smoke and fire of the Civil War. By gazing into these years and watching how the young warrior would develop, it is easy to identify certain character traits that would actually help the Little Bighorn disaster unfold.

Finally, it is my intention in this book to focus on his personality and how he chose to conduct war. Therefore, I will not be following his life in a sequential sense, detailing every battle and skirmish, as other biographers have done so splendidly. Rather, I have chosen to look closely into his overall attitude and reactions to those battles. By doing so, the inevitable path to Little Big Horn becomes terribly clear.

Even so, the failings of one campaign, no matter how blatant, cannot erase the courage displayed or the accomplishments he achieved during the Civil War. It is also good to remember that, like the rest of humanity, Custer was a complex individual and sometimes given to extremes. Yet in many ways, I see the complexities of his life amplified, and I have come to see his personality as one vastly different from most individuals one would expect to encounter in life. Indeed, in my years of studying, I have often found myself drifting somewhere between respect and disgust for the man. And perhaps, in light of the evidence, this is the way it ought to be.

Kevin M. Sullivan
Louisville, Kentucky

Chapter One

TRUE HEART OF THE WARRIOR

George Armstrong Custer was born on December 5, 1839, to Emmanuel and Maria Custer, in the small town of New Rumley, Ohio. Relatively speaking, his life would be very brief, ending in his thirty-seventh year. Yet, even within this short period of time, Custer would leave his mark on the world as few others have.

From the time of his youth Custer possessed a robust, if not uncommon physical stamina. Even at the time of his death he had more physical endurance than many of the troops he commanded. In photographs, however, he often appeared older, having a weathered or worn-out look. But here the camera lied, for Custer would continue to possess an almost furious physical stamina right up until the very end.

When Custer entered West Point Military Academy in July, 1857, he was not yet eighteen years of age. Over the next four years his scholastic performance would be anything but spectacular, and he would end his years there by graduating thirty-fourth in a class of thirty-four. Years later, even he would concede that his days as a cadet "had but little to recommend it to the study of those who came after me, unless as an example to be carefully avoided." [1] Custer's failure to distinguish himself in the classroom may have caused some of his peers to snicker, if only in private moments. But in a very short time, the reputation of George Custer would rocket ahead of all of his classmates, forever granting him his place of prominence in the class of 1861.

That he would excel on the battlefield and not at West Point is understandable, given his type of personality. The classroom was not his element, nor was it the arena in which his personality could thrive. Custer needed West Point not so much for what it could teach him, but for where it would take him. For Custer, it was not important to gain scholastic honors while at the academy; this is obvious. Nevertheless, he possessed the abilities, both physical and mental, to graduate from West Point, and this he did on June 24, 1861. In fact, he closed his books just as war with the South was igniting. And having discarded his pen—at least for a time—he took up his sword and galloped towards the destiny which awaited him. His most glorious years were just ahead.

But just as his lack of drive for the classroom was ending, his desire to taste the sweet fruits that the battlefield had to offer were increasing. Here, the element was as cold as steel, and Custer loved it. And it would be here, among the booming of cannon and the screams of the wounded, that George Custer would find his place in life. Once discovered, this realm of violence would remain pre-eminent in his life, ascending in importance over all the other affairs of his life. Only death itself would release him from this iron grip of a commitment. Evidently, no risk was too great, nor was any danger too severe. The fear of death, the fear of being maimed, the loss of the future, even his 1864 marriage to Elizabeth Bacon could not restrain him from his fellowship with war. West Point provided him with the uniform of a soldier, but it could not provide him with the heart of a warrior; this he already possessed. The letters he wrote from the field provide an interesting glimpse into the heart of George A. Custer. The letters were personal, and therefore it is certain that he never imagined they would ever be seen by the public. Yet many of these letters were saved for posterity, giving us today a good picture—albeit a literary one—of how young Custer felt about and adapted to the warfare that swirled around him.

For Custer, the Civil War held out to him the promise of a twofold blessing. First, it provided him with the atmosphere he desired most. Young Custer would never shrink from battle. On the contrary, he would always gallop towards it. He was like a magnet being drawn by the sound of the guns. Second, he was acutely aware that should he be fortunate enough to survive the war, he might well come out of it with a great name, and it was his desire to capitalize on that name after hostilities ceased.[2] As his personal letters revealed, Custer found pleasure in the sights of sounds of combat, strangely referring to cavalry charges as "beautiful" and "glorious".[3] After one particular charge the young warrior confesses that he never expected to see a "...prettier sight."[4] Such fond expressions of battle are usually reserved for those who have never tasted war. But G.A.C. already had two years of battle under his belt, and had seen plenty of bloodletting when he penned these words. He goes on to describe one charge in particular and how he would repeatedly turn in his saddle "...to see the glittering sabres advance in the sunlight."[5] Never mind that these same glittering sabres would soon be hacking away at human flesh; severing arteries, nerves, and families forever. Never mind all that! War, for this young cavalry officer, was beautiful, and no amount of human agony connected with it would take away from its splendor. This is the heart of the warrior, and it was very much at the center of Custer's being.

Custer's bravery under fire was nothing short of legendary. Always at the head of his men, he would charge into battle with an intensity that would stay constant throughout his life. If he ever experienced fear while on the battlefield it must have been minimal indeed. Certainly not the paralyzing type that keeps one from performing one's duties. Had he experienced such crippling fear it certainly would have surfaced in his actions, but as his distinguished military record reveals, this was not the case. He sincerely loved combat and would hurl himself at the enemy at every opportunity. Such zeal often leads to extinction, of course, but in Custer's case it was always the man beside him, or behind him, who was sent reeling into oblivion. And while Custer was indeed a skilled cavalryman, in such heated hand-to-hand contests, skill will only take you so far and can guarantee you nothing. Here, the brave, the coward, the swift, and the slow, can all die together. As the corpses piled up, they would make room for privates and generals alike, yet Custer was never among them.

It was also very important for Custer to have officers serving under him who were of like nature. In describing one young officer—a Captain Green—Custer writes of taking him to a place where the rebel bullets were coming in "thick and fast." Obviously watching him closely for any sign of fear, Custer was pleased that "...He never faltered, was as calm and collected as if sitting at dinner." [6]

For such a man as Custer, promotions were sure to come. By the summer of 1863, while serving with General Alfred Plesenton, Lieutenant Custer became Brigadier General of the Michigan Volunteers. Although a brevet (or temporary) rank, it was an honor that stilled the hoots and hollers of those who chided Custer for ever boasting that he would wear a general's star. Promotion to Major General came on October 23, 1864. Custer, fresh from the victory at Cedar Creek, Virginia, where he routed the famous rebel Jubel Early, had come to Washington with his men to present Secretary of War Edwin Stanton with thirteen captured Confederate flags. And while capturing enemy flags in this century means little more than having a fine souvenir, in Custer's day they were prized possessions. In fact, it was not only considered a great honor to capture a flag from the enemy, but it was just as great an honor to be allowed to carry one's own flag into battle.

Being promoted to the rank of general gave Custer not only the opportunity to command more men, but also would have allowed him to draw back somewhat from those almost suicidal charges he would often engage in. But it must be remembered that Custer would attack the enemy with such aggression not to obtain the stars of a general, but because this was his style of conducting battle. Although his rank would evolve throughout the war, his tactics would not. And his military exploits—exploits many would call rash and reckless—would justifiably give him honor and distinction granted to only a few. For many, Custer was the ideal warrior.

As can be expected, he was immensely popular with many of the men throughout his command. Private Victor E. Comte, who was serving as personal escort for Custer during the battle of Falling Waters in July 1863, would later write "...I saw him plunge his sabre into the belly of a rebel who was trying to kill him. You can guess how bravely soldiers fight for such a General." [7] Major James H. Kidd said of Custer: "We swear by his name. His name is our battle cry. He can get twice the fight out of this brigade than any man possibly can do." [8]

But not all who served with the boy-General were as enamored of him. Seventh Cavalry Private Theodore Ewert felt Custer's bravado stemmed from something other than pure motives: "The hardships and danger to his men, as well as the probable loss of life were worthy of but little considerations when dim visions of an eagle or even a star floated before the excited mind of our Lt. Colonel." [9] Another Seventh Cavalry trooper, Corporal Jacob Horner, believed G.A.C. was far too hard on man and beast, adding sarcastically: "He was always right. He never conferred enough with his officers, when he got a notion, we had to go." [10] And go they did.

Almost as surprising as Custer surviving the war was his surviving it virtually intact. His most serious wound occurred at Culpeper Court House in September, 1863. While he was leading a charge an artillery shell exploded, sending a hot piece of shrapnel through Custer's thigh, killing his horse.

Ironically, the luck which carried Custer safely in and out of battle would not extend to the beasts supporting him. During the fighting at Gettysburg in July 1863, G.A.C. lost three horses while engaging the army of Robert E. Lee. On another occasion, two of the very large targets crumpled under him within the span of only fifteen minutes. But the bullets would not always strike the horse. On one occasion a rebel bullet nearly ended the career of the boy-general by clipping off a lock of his hair. During another fight he was hit twice but the bullets, having lost nearly all their power caused only minor bruises and swelling.[11] Seemingly, there was no end to the luck of young General Custer. At least his luck would not end here, during this conflict, and with this enemy.

Regardless of how one may feel about this wonder warrior—whether you love him or hate him—one thing cannot be denied: from the first Battle of Bull Run to the decisive cavalry charges immediately preceding the surrender at Appomattox, George Armstrong Custer left one of the most exemplary, courageous, and distinguished records to emerge from the Civil War. No matter what mistakes were made at Little Bighorn, Custer left a Civil War record that continues to shine brightly today. Hence, it is extremely unfortunate that he is judged so severely overall because of the events of June 25-26, 1876. In judging Custer, it is very important to view the man not by any one particular incident, as some have chosen to do, but by the overall record and how his personality evolved during those years. Yet even when one looks at the facts of a particular incident, the picture has a tendency sometimes to become very murky. To understand the sequence of events in any given situation in life, one cannot always know the true intentions or feelings of those involved. Actions can tell us the facts of a situation, but they cannot reveal motive.

An excellent example of where I believe Custer has been judged harshly—but wrongly—was the now famous story of the killing of the Confederate officer. The incident occurred in 1862, while Custer was serving with his old regiment, the Fifth Cavalry. Having charged a rebel gun emplacement near White Oak Swamp—which immediately broke and ran— Custer, on the heels of a fleeing confederate, shouted out a command for the man to surrender. When Custer heard no response, he shouted out the command to surrender once more, but this, too, proved in vain. Custer fired his pistol at him but missed. A second shot found its mark, knocking the gray-clad officer from his saddle. Custer was galloping so quickly that he flew past the crumpled form upon the ground and could not see what happened next. According to Lieutenant Byrnes, the mortally wounded rebel "...rose to his feet, turned around, threw up his hands and fell to the ground with a stream of blood gushing from his mouth." [12]

Because Custer had described the horse that carried the officer as "splendid,"[13] and because he chose to shoot the man instead of the horse, this is given as proof of his callousness. Never mind that it was the man who was the danger to Custer and not the horse. One thing is certain: when the fleeing officer ignored Custer's order to stop, a violent end was assured. Writing later of the incident, Custer put the responsibility squarely on the rebel officer who obviously desired escape so he might fight another day. His wounding evidently caused him to change his mind, but the bullet had struck a vital area, and death—not surrender—was now only seconds away. That G.A.C. would later describe this encounter as if it had been an exciting hunt means absolutely nothing. Veterans have been doing this for as long as there have been wars. After all, in Custer's mind, it was more than a mere contest, seeing that he held out the opportunity for his opponent to surrender. His decision to extend this mercy could have easily resulted in his own death. Any person who has ever experienced combat understands that it is at such moments, when you hold back from using force, that everything can go wrong. As an experienced combat veteran, Custer knew this very well.

Callousness did exist within the heart of George Custer, but it was not a callousness which was directed at any particular individual, nor could it be defined by any one particular incident. The callousness which pervaded his life was an emotional detachment from the results of battle, results that could just as easily include himself. The harsh price which is extracted from those who participate in war simply did not bother him. Instead of fearing death, Custer became emotionally attached to that activity which offered death at every turn. In this respect, Custer must be considered a part of that strange breed of warrior who is the exception rather than the rule for those who participate in combat. Indeed, such emotional divorce from the slaughter of fellow humans strikes most of us as bizarre. And those few individuals who do exhibit the love for battle, live on the other side of the line, so to speak, a line which the majority of humanity will never cross, nor even have a desire to do so.

Throughout history, countless millions have marched off to wars, and those fortunate enough to return physically would sometimes later find that their emotional return to normal life and society was far more difficult to achieve. Many souls are never able to overcome the extreme violence and carnage which is always a by-product of the battlefield. But only a handful who march off to war actually love it. To look fondly on such inhumane activity borders on the insane. Yet Custer truly loved this environment. Had he not been slain in the summer of 1876, he no doubt would have continued in this arena for some time to come. I say this not to be critical of his personality, I mention it merely as an observation. George Armstrong Custer was first and foremost a soldier, and as a soldier he both loved and felt comfortable performing his duties, be it in a time of war or peace. He always understood the risks involved, and he was willing to pay the ultimate price should it be asked of him. Yes, this was his duty as a soldier, but it was a duty he loved above all things. Indeed, it was his sole reason for living.

Several years ago General H. Norman Schwarzkopf returned to his former battlefields in Vietnam. As he was being interviewed by Dan Rather of CBS News, he confessed that during the war he had seen fellow officers, graduates of the military academy, so fearful of mine fields that they dug foxholes, jumped in, and refused to come out again.[14] Had Custer been standing next to Schwarzkopf during this time, such paralyzing fear would have been unforgivable. I am sure that Custer would have regarded these individuals as a disgrace to the officer corps, and would not even have looked upon them as soldiers.

On July 8, 1876, while in Philadelphia, General William Sherman received a telegram from General Philip H. Sheridan which included these words: "I deeply deplore the loss of Custer and his officers and men. I fear it was an unnecessary sacrifice, due to misapprehension and superabundance of courage, the latter extraordinarily developed in Custer." [15] Of course, during the Civil War, Sheridan loved this superabundance of courage which, as he said, was so extraordinarily developed in Custer. But that was before the egregious disaster at Little Bighorn, and with so many lives lost in what was clearly a military defeat, I suppose it is natural to point the finger at the dead who cannot speak. Had Little Bighorn been a rousing success, with the Indians crumpling in defeat instead of the mighty Seventh Cavalry, Custer's superiors would have once again been heard singing the praises of the bold Lieutenant Colonel George Armstrong Custer, no matter how rash his actions might have been. How easy it is to rally around the victors in life. Yet no one wants to rally around the defeated dead. How predictable—and laughable—the nature of the human species can be.

Custer entered the Civil War as an obscure figure among many thousands who shared the same unglamorous position. Yet he exited the most brutal and bloody war ever waged on the continent a true American hero. His status as a fearless warrior was assured. Whatever else he might accomplish in life, he would always be remembered—and loved—for his exploits during the war that preserved the Union. The year 1865 must have felt good to Custer. He had come through the violence alive and in one piece. Whatever lay ahead could never match what the Civil War had to offer. Or could it?

In late December 1866, an incident occurred which probably sent a chill up Custer's back. I mention it here because of the similarities between this incident—and the individual responsible for it—and Custer's mistakes at the Battle of Little Bighorn a decade later. It should have been viewed as a warning to Custer, a sober reminder of what can occur if things go wrong, no matter who the enemy might be. However, the truth of the matter failed to penetrate Custer's heart, and did not produce the necessary caution that could have aided him in his decision-making at Little Bighorn. Most likely, the following story was considered by him to be little more than a collection of unhappy facts of an unlucky fellow officer whose fate will be remembered, and deposited, in that metaphorical book of military disasters. Little did he know that his name would some day be added to this inglorious list, and that his beloved Seventh Cavalry would have a prominent chapter all to itself.

Anyway, on December 21, 1866, Captain William J. Fetterman, accompanied by a force of eighty men, rushed out of Ft. Phil Kearney to aid in the deliverance of the wood train that was once again under attack by the Indians. Ft. Phil Kearney, located near the present-day town of Sheridan, Wyoming, was a hotbed of activity, and the Indians had become very adept at killing these blue-coated soldiers. December 21 would prove to be an especially good day for the persistent Indians.

The commanding officer of the fort, Colonel Henry B. Carrington, was forty-three years old and displayed the type of caution one might expect to find in a man of middle age. Carrington also recognized the rash nature which boiled within the heart of the young captain. Like Custer, Fetterman enjoyed battle and had seen plenty of action fighting the Confederates. Also like Custer, he felt that the U.S. military could always whip the Indians, no matter how great their numbers.

Before Fetterman's troops dashed out of the safety of the fort, Carrington's orders were clear. He was not to attack the Indians, but was to support the wood train only. "Under no circumstances pursue over the ridge, that is, Lodge Trail Ridge."[16] Carrington must have sensed that Fetterman would disobey, as he sent a Lieutenant Wands to repeat the order before the doomed command was out of the gate. Yet within a short time, Captain Fetterman would cross Lodge Trail Ridge and Carrington would be powerless to stop him.

Acting as decoys, a small party of warriors were successful in coaxing Fetterman to chase them to a spot—over Lodge Trail Ridge, of course,—where they would all be overwhelmed and killed. One of the young warriors in this group was an Oglala by the name of Crazy Horse, who, ten years later, would play an important role in the death of Custer. Dying with Fetterman was fellow officer Captain Frederick Brown, a man who was as much out for Indian blood as Fetterman himself. Just before their position was about to be overrun, the besieged captains, not wishing to fall into the Indians' hands while still alive, placed their revolvers to one another's heads and fired. So ended what became known as the Fetterman Massacre. Only the Custer debacle would shock the nation more.

As soon as was possible, Carrington dispatched a rider to Ft. Laramie with a telegram to be sent to General Crook. After an explanation concerning the disaster and asking for reinforcements, stating that he intended to hold the fort at all costs, Carrington ended his message with the emotional statement: "The Indians desperate, and they spare none." [17]

Such was the nature of the war in the West.

Chapter Two

WHEN WORLDS COLLIDE

From the moment the first white European set foot on the land which later would be called the United States of America, the fate of the American Indian was sealed. To be sure, hundreds of years would pass before the final curtain would fall at a place called Wounded Knee in the winter of 1890. But it would surely come, for the wheels of European thinking would always turn in the direction of progress. And the progress that was coming would mean change such as the land had never imagined. The Indians, whose strange nomadic ways were regarded by the whites as something out of the stone age, were an obstacle that could be tolerated only so long. Yet it would prove to be a long struggle, filled with broken hearts and broken promises, where lives were shattered and lives were enriched, depending on the color of one's skin. The newer, stronger culture showed through experience that what could not be had through the lying of the tongue, could—and would—be obtained through the impact of a bullet. It would be harsh and unrelenting, and there would be no salvation for those outside of the fold.

As one historian so correctly stated: "Whites had steadily encroached upon Indian Lands, and new treaties of cessation had been negotiated from time to time to validate the incursions." [1] Whenever humanitarians would cry out concerning the ill treatment of the Indian, such attempts "…Ultimatly foundered on the deep seated conviction that the white man had a superior right to the land." [2]

When George A. Custer entered this great drama it would be in the latter years of struggle, in what was truly the winter of the Indians' discontent. Having blazed a path of glory through the Civil War, Custer was ready to answer that westward call and the glory that would come from fighting a new enemy. But fame and glory, always an important aspect to G.A.C., would not follow him as closely or as faithfully as it had in the war of rebellion. Indeed, Custer's most famous encounter with these "children of nature" as they were sometimes called, would end in one of the most humiliating defeats ever suffered by the United States military. Custer's only other major engagement with the red race occurred along the Washita River in late November, 1868. If this battle were a victory at all for the general, then it was a somewhat poisoned one, for long after the last shot was fired, or the last arrow launched, the Battle of the Washita would continue to have an effect on all of those involved. The Cheyenne would never forget what was done to their sleeping village, and neither would certain elements within the Seventh Cavalry. In fact, Custer's actions at Washita would be a bone of contention within the ranks that would clearly separate those who saw Custer as a hero, from those who considered him an uncaring, opportunistic brute whose greatest interest would always be directed towards himself. For the Cheyenne, the battle would hold a special irony. Their Chief, Black Kettle, a well-known advocate of peace with the United States, barely escaped death when troops under the command of Colonel John M. Chivington attacked his camp at Sand Creek on November 28, 1864. Although he flew an American flag over his village, this would make little difference to those determined to destroy his camp.

Chivington, a former minister, tossed aside his Bible to kill Confederates during the Civil War. Before attacking Black Kettle's village he gave this instruction: "Kill and scalp all big and little. Nits make lice."[3] In complete obedience to the "Fighting Parson," as he was called, his troops responded with a zest and determination that would make any bloodthirsty ghoul proud. Without hesitation, little children were killed while begging for their lives, some were shot, others had their heads bashed in with the butts of rifles. All of this was done with the approval of the colonel, although later on, Chivington would disavow ever having any knowledge that such atrocities occurred. How one evolves from minister to child-killer is beyond me, but he did, and before the firing stopped, over three hundred Cheyenne were dead, two-thirds of them women and children.

Those who participated in the attack would refer to Sand Creek as a battle, but as the grisly details spread to the outside world, this battle would receive its proper and final name: The Sand Creek Massacre. Even so, Chivington would defend his actions all the way to the grave.

Black Kettle, who managed to escape the hail of bullets at Sand Creek, would find his second nightmare in the form of George Custer. This time, however, Black Kettle would not be as lucky as he was at Sand Creek. Both he and his wife would fall under the barrage of bullets unleashed by the Seventh Cavalry. Oddly, Custer's attack upon Black Kettle's village occurred almost four years to the day after Sand Creek.

Because of raids that were being carried out by various bands of Indians—depredations that were in part caused by the Sand Creek slaughter—General Philip Sheridan dispatched troops to crush the Indians.

Custer began his trek into the wilderness on November 23, 1868. During the previous night the weather, as if allied with the Indians, dropped over a foot of snow on the blue-coated hunters. Some of the troopers were no doubt dreading their march into this winter wonderland, but not Custer. He was certain the snow would work in their favor, greatly reducing the possibility of a move on the part of the Indians. Even General Sheridan was calmed by Custer's confidence.

The Nineteenth Kansas Volunteer Cavalry, commanded by former Kansas Governor Samuel J. Crawford, was to accompany Custer on this famous campaign but was thwarted by the heavy snow. Having departed Topeka on the fifth of November, the troops were destined to endure a brutal ordeal. Though spared the danger of Indian warfare, Crawford would nevertheless have his hands full battling the elements. Not until the twenty-seventh of November—the day before the Washita battle would occur—would the weary and frozen Nineteenth Kansas enter base supply.

While the Nineteenth Kansas struggled, Custer was having his own problems. Not only was the snow straining both man and beast, whatever trail which may have been left by a recent war party was now under eighteen inches of snow. It continued to come down, and at some point early in the march, the Osage guides were unable to direct the command due to the blinding snow. Even terrain ordinarily familiar to them was unrecognizable in the maze of white. Not to be deterred, Custer decided to lead the command himself through the use of a compass.

On November 25, having had no luck on their present course, Custer changed direction and headed towards the Antelope Hills, reaching the Canadian Valley by nightfall.

Early the next morning, Major Elliott, with companies G, H, and M, rode off in search of any telltale signs made by any war parties who, if still out, must surely be heading back to their winter camps. Meanwhile, the rest of the command was kept busy getting across the icy South Canadian River. Thanks to the old scout California Joe, they were able to find a suitable place for the troops to cross, a crossing which only took three hours. As Custer was about to get the regiment moving again, he spied a rider far off in the distance plodding as fast as possible on the snow-encrusted plain. Soon the rider came into focus and it was none other than the scout Jack Corbin, bringing news from the now-distant Elliott. Like lightning, Custer's mind danced with imagination. What could Elliott have found? Had he located a trail, as Custer so desperately wanted? Or had he come up empty-handed and dispatched Corbin back to the main command for further orders? One can easily imagine the adrenaline rush Custer must have experienced as Corbin approached with what the boy-general hoped would be good news. For within Custer's heart, only the promise of an imminent battle would please him.

Corbin did bring him the news he most wanted to hear: Major Elliott had indeed discovered the trail of a war party numbering between one hundred and one hundred fifty. Elated, Custer asked Corbin if he thought he could overtake Elliott if provided with a fresh mount. Corbin acknowledged that he could indeed, and soon the lone scout rode off into the blinding whiteness which stretched out before him. Corbin had orders to tell the major that he was to continue the chase, but that if Custer had not caught up with him by nightfall, he was to stop and wait until the command could be joined.

Custer realized that to have any real chance of catching Elliott, he would have to cut himself loose from the burdensome, slow-moving wagons. This he did, leaving eighty troopers to guard it under the command of the officer of the day, with orders to join the command as quickly as possible.

On this day, the officer of the day was Captain Louis McLane Hamilton. Young Hamilton, a grandson of the famous American Alexander Hamilton, was only twenty-three years old as he made this march to the Washita on a cold November day. That he was about to be left behind while his own company charged into battle did not sit well with the brave captain. Desiring to extricate himself from what he perceived as an unfortunate situation, Hamilton sought out Custer in the hope that he would change the order. While sympathizing with him, Custer was not about to force this duty on any one else, although he did agree, should Hamilton find a replacement on his own, to allow him to accompany the main command into battle. Hamilton, who was very persistent in his search, convinced Second Lieutenant Edward Mathey, who was suffering from snow blindness, to remain behind as officer of the day. Unknown to young Hamilton, his fate was now sealed. If it were not for this unbelievable (in Hamilton's mind) stroke of luck, he might also have lived to become a grandfather. But all of this had now changed, and Louis McLane Hamilton was now in the last hours of his life.

By 9 p.m., Custer was finally able to reach Major Elliott, who, like Hamilton, was now in the last hours of his life as well. Elliott had made camp near a stream adjacent to a timbered valley. The stream had deep banks which allowed the troops to build fires for coffee and remain out of sight.

However, this much-needed rest for man and beast would be very short. By 10 p.m.—and without the customary bugle calls—the regiment was again on the move. The Indian scouts had assured Custer that the camp of the enemy could not be very far away.

Leading the column on foot three or four hundred yards in advance were the two Osage scouts whose natural skill and ability obviously fascinated Custer. Later on he would write: "...they were our guides and the Panther, creeping upon its prey could not have advanced more cautiously or quietly than did these friendly Indians." Making reference to the strange, almost supernatural quality of their movements, he added: "They seemed to glide rather than walk over the snow clad surface." [4]

Behind the two dismounted scouts rode Custer with the other Osage and white scouts. The rest of the command rode four abreast, sometimes as far back as one-half mile. Custer wanted this distance to minimize the chance of the Indians being alerted to their presence by the sound of hundreds of horses hoofs crunching through the snow. Strict orders had been given that no communication was to be above a whisper, neither were those given to the use of tobacco allowed to indulge themselves on this raw, cold evening. Custer was determined that the command remain undetected during this hunt.

Soon their nocturnal trek would be halted when the two Osage scouts stopped. When Custer rode up to ask what was the matter, one of the scouts responded in broken English,

"Me don't know, but me smell fire."[5] Just then, several officers came out from the darkness to hear what the Indians had to say. As there was no white nose in the group that could perceive anything close to the smell of a fire, they concluded the Osage was mistaken. In minutes the column was again on the move but after traveling only one mile the Osage again stopped and Custer was again summoned. "Me told you so,"[6] the Osage whispered, pointing out the dying embers of a small fire. After investigation it was determined that it must have been used by those watching over the pony herds earlier.

Custer followed one of the guides to the crest of the hill. While he stared out into the cold, dark night he saw what appeared to be a mass of animals, but what they were he could not tell. The guide said he heard a dog bark, which could be a very good sign as the Indians were known to have many of them. Soon another dog was heard barking, followed by a tinkling of a bell—another good sign, for it was the custom of the Indians to hang a bell from the lead pony.

Custer, convinced the prey lay just before him, was already retracing his steps from the crest of the hill when he heard the wail of a child echoing from the valley below. While this cry of an innocent did not deter him from his mission, he did acknowledge regret "that in a war such as we were forced to engage in the mode and circumstance of battle would possibly prevent discrimination."[7]

Now certain, Custer hurriedly assembled his officers together. After having them quietly stack their sabres—he did not want any unnecessary clanging of metal—he took them to the crest of the hill. Unknown to the sleeping Cheyenne village, their enemy was now beholding them and were almost ready to strike. Recalling the scene years later, Colonel Albert Barnitz said, "We all crept very quietly and slowly to the top of the ridge...And I could not help thinking that we very much resembled a pack of wolves." [8]

After returning to where they had stacked their sabres, Custer informed them of his intention to completely surround the village before the attack. After splitting his command into four detachments, Custer used the remaining hours of darkness getting everyone into position. Because of the distance that they would have to cover just to get into their positions by dawn, two detachments departed immediately. A third began their role in the encirclement one hour before dawn.

The morning air was extremely cold and Custer had ordered that no fires were to be made. Neither could anyone stamp their feet in an effort to keep warm. While the Cheyenne slept soundly, the blue-coats readied themselves for war. On this night, Custer would sleep barely one hour.

Before morning, a strange apparition appeared that left Custer certain that the enemy had discovered them and were even now raising a signal of alarm. What appeared to be a rocket rising slowly above the doomed village was nothing but the brilliance of a morning star filling the cold night air. Custer said it displayed "The most beautiful combination of prismatic tints," [9] adding that it would remain a topic of conversation among Seventh Cavalry officers for years to come.

As daylight could now be seen breaking out in the east, Custer gave the order to advance. Although the troopers were already bitterly cold, he ordered that haversacks and overcoats were to be removed so as not to encumber the men during battle. This no doubt was met with a variety of internal curses, especially among the enlisted troops, as they laid their overcoats and equipment on the snowy ground.

The regiment was now completely separated and Custer earnestly hoped that everyone was in place now that the attack was ready to begin. Besides the mounted troops, Custer had wisely chosen forty sharpshooters under the command of Lieutenant W.W. Cooke. They were to walk into battle, situating themselves among the trees at the rivers edge, for better firing accuracy. Here they would have a good view of the battle and would be able to unleash a steady hail of lead against the warriors as they emerged from their tepees.

Custer led the column as the troops descended the long slope leading to the river. Directly across lay the sleeping Cheyenne encampment. Captain Louis Hamilton, who had fought so hard to accompany the regiment was overheard encouraging his men to "keep cool and fire low." By now they were near enough to see the white tepees of the still undisturbed village. Just as Custer was about to give the signal for the band to begin playing the musical battle cry of the Seventh Cavalry, "Garry Owen," the sound of a rifle shot from the opposite end of the camp erupted in the morning air. The attack was now on! Custer waved his hand and for a few seconds the sound of "Garry Owen" filled the valley floor, but again the elements would reign supreme, instantly freezing the men's saliva rendering the instruments useless. What could not be silenced, however, were the cheers and the shouts of the men sweeping down on the camp from all sides.

Unknown to Custer, the rifle shot came from an Indian "wrapped in a red blanket..." [10] who had discovered the troopers as he was guarding a herd of ponies and mules. This startled Cheyenne wasted no time getting back into camp to sound the alarm. Even so, the camp would quickly fall to Custer's four-pronged attack.

Charging down on the camp with G.A.C. were companies A, D, K, and C, while Cooke and his sharpshooters fanned out to the general's left towards the tree-lined river's edge. Major Elliott, with companies G, H, and M, struck the camp to the left of Custer, while Captain Edward Meyers, with companies E and I, attacked on Custer's right. Captain Thompson with companies B and F, hit the camp almost directly in the rear, as did Lieutenant Godfrey with Troop K, whose orders were to rush through the village and seize the invaluable pony herd.

As always, Custer was at the head of his men as they rushed down the slope. Quickly clearing the Washita River, Custer encountered a warrior with a rifle and immediately sent a bullet into his head. After running another down with his horse, he took up a position on a slight hill where he could oversee the fighting, giving orders as needed.

When Captain Frederick W. Benteen came charging into the pandemonium that was now Black Kettle's camp, he encountered an Indian boy that he supposed was not more than fourteen years old. Not regarding him as a warrior, Benteen began making hand signals indicating that the boy should surrender, but the youth had other ideas. As Benteen held his fire, the young Cheyenne sent a bullet past the captain's head. At this point, almost any other member of the Seventh Cavalry would have gladly killed the boy, but not the cool-headed captain, who continued to hold his fire. Two more shots were fired; the second of which struck Benteen's horse in the neck, hurling him into the snow. Enough was enough. Benteen's pistol cracked and the boy fell dead. The lifeless form was Blue Horse, a nephew of Black Kettle.

That Benteen allowed his opponent to shoot three times before firing the fatal shot revealed his sincere desire to spare the boy's life. Even so, it would remain a source of regret to the captain for years to come.

Throughout the camp the disorganized sounds of battle filled the air: the shouts of the war cry, the pitiful screams of the children who could not fathom why such violence had come to their homes, and the unmistakable wail of the wounded which can follow a direct hit.

A young Indian girl named Moving Behind, who was only fourteen years old at the time of the battle, said years later how difficult it was for anyone to escape the heavy firing being unleashed from the troopers' weapons: "The air was full of smoke from gunfire... we could see the red fire of the shots." [11] The entire valley must have been filled with the smell of burnt gunpowder. While hiding in the grass, Moving

Behind could easily hear the groanings of the wounded ponies and recalled how human-like were their cries.

Attacking with Benteen's column was Colonel Albert Barnitz. Although an able soldier, Barnitz did not share Benteen's sympathy for the Indians. Barnitz recalled how his troops came face to face with a group of Cheyenne fleeing the opposite end of the camp, and how a number of these were immediately killed, while the remainder were driven to a nearby ravine where they were later cut down.

When Barnitz and Major Elliott spotted another group running towards the pony herds, the order was given to fire. But when none of the Cheyenne were seen to drop, Sergeant McDermot and some men were ordered to give chase. When Barnitz caught up with these Indians he discovered that they were only women and children and "...not caring to waste ammunition on them..." decided to hold his fire.[12]

Barnitz would find himself in a sort of a duel with an Indian just minutes later. Having tried numerous times, but failing to situate himself in a good position in which to fire on the warrior, shots rang out from both parties at almost point-blank range. Although Barnitz' pistol had found its mark, so had the Indian's old Lancaster rifle (that shot, being so close, actually left a burn mark on Barnitz' coat). Unknown to the colonel, the bullet entered his left side and exited his right side without doing any significant, long-lasting damage. Yet when Doctors Lipponcott and Renick examined him, they declared the wound to be fatal. Even Custer, who had seen hundreds of men expire in battle, felt that he had but minutes to live:"…his face wore that pale deathly aspect so common and peculiar to those mortally wounded."[13]

When Dr. Lipponcott dispatched Lieutenant Godfrey to carry the message to Barnitz that his recovery was in doubt, Barnitz, feeling far more optimistic, blurted out, "Oh hell! They think because my extremities are cold I am going to die, but if I could get warm I'm sure I'll be alright."[14] Barnitz was right, death would not come to him for many years.

For the most part, the Cheyenne were being overwhelmed—either killed or captured. However, a few souls were able to escape through a gap in the lines. Major Elliott, not willing that any should escape, took up the chase along with nineteen other troopers. Benteen later would describe Elliott's adventure as going "…off on his own hook." Indeed, Lieutenant Hale overheard Elliott shout out "Here goes for a Brevet or a coffin," just before the chase began. But there would be no promotion for the major at the end of this ride. The Indians they were galloping after were quickly joined by other warriors from the various camps along the Washita. The opposing force would prove too great for Elliott's command, and within a very short time all were killed and subsequently mutilated.

Custer, completely unaware of the number of villages in the area, was soon informed by Lieutenant Godfrey that while his company was gathering up the pony herds, he had taken some time to scout the land east of the village where he found an even larger body of warriors. When the general first heard Godfrey's report he exclaimed, " What's that ?" But as the

Lieutenant explained,"What's that" became very clear to him. After Godfrey had spied the body of dismounted Indians running down the opposite end of the valley, he quickly turned over the captured ponies to Lieutenant Law and gave chase. Obviously, Godfrey was being driven by the same type of fatal thinking which had taken Elliott to his death. In any event, the platoon pressed onward.

After clearing the stream, Godfrey followed the Indians' trail, locating them, now mounted, in a wooded draw where a larger pony herd had been concealed. Following the trail on the hills rising above the valley, Godfrey passed by a lone tepee. Just beyond were seen two mounted Indians riding in a circle. "I knew the circling of the warriors meant an alarm and rally, but I wanted to see what was in the valley beyond them." [16]

Godfrey's unbridled rashness was soon tempered by the warnings of two veteran sergeants, Conrad and Hughes, concerning the dangers of continuing on. Leaving the rest of the men, Godfrey climbed a nearby ridge to obtain a better view. "I was amazed to find that as far as I could see...there were tepees—tepees." [17] Not only that, but as was the case with Major Elliott, warriors were coming to meet them. Godfrey's troops were forced to fight a retreating action all the way back to Black Kettle's conquered village. Luckily, they would suffer no casualties in their hurried withdrawal.

As the hills surrounding the camp began to sprout warriors, it appears the immensity of what could be out there began to play on the mind of Custer. As time was of the essence, Custer now turned his attention to the task of turning the camp to rubble. Tepees, buffalo robes, anything combustible was now torched. Custer would, however, carry away, and later present to a Michigan historical society, an ornate Cheyenne shield, and the scalp of the warrior who carried it. And the ponies, which Custer had ordered gathered up and numbered as many as eight hundred, were killed as well.

Later on, when G.A.C. put to pen his adventures on the plains, he greatly enlarged the size of the Indian force confronting him. It was this, as well as other inconsistences, which led Captain F. W. Benteen to refer to Custer's book *My Life On The Plains* as "My Lie On The Plains." In fact, Benteen was so enraged by Custer's refusal to conduct a proper search for Elliott and his men that he wrote a friend in St Louis, giving him a detailed account of Custer's handling of the Washita affair. Little did Benteen realize that his now famous letter would wind up being published in the *St Louis Democrat* and then the *New York Times*. The published letter bore no signature, however, as Benteen's friend had sent it in anonymously.

When Custer got wind of it he became hopping mad, and he was more than determined to confront and chasten the writer, or writers, of this treacherous slap in the face.

Custer got his chance at Fort Cobb. Having assembled his officers together in his tent, Custer walked back and forth in the tent's center, all the while breathing out threats and the promise of a whipping should he find the person responsible.

Evidently, Custer was intent on making his point quite clear as he held in his hand the tool of punishment—a rawhide riding crop—the entire time. Little did he know that his intended dressing down was about to backfire in his face, ending in his own humiliation.

Benteen, who like Custer, never seemed to exhibit fear, and who was not about to be castigated by anyone in the matter, decided to respond to the general's offer. After listening to Custer's tirade from the doorway of the tent, Benteen simply stepped outside long enough to check his revolver, making sure it was in good working order. Returning inside, Benteen waited until there was an appropriate pause before blurting out, "General Custer, while I cannot father all of the blame you have asserted, still, I guess I am the man you are after, and I am ready for the whipping promised." [18] At this, Custer began to stammer (a common occurrence whenever he became excited) and could only respond "Colonel Benteen, I'll see you again, sir." As Benteen alluded years later: "…had the rawhide whirred…" as he put it, the confrontation certainly would have turned violent.[19] Of course, shooting Custer would have been extreme, to say the least. Still, there is no reason to doubt Benteen's claim of instant and fatal retribution had Custer delivered the promised whipping. Even so, Benteen would always perform his soldierly duties well and at no time would he look for ways to undercut Custer or show disrespect for his rank. His dislike of Custer—a dislike which increased significantly after Washita—would not sway him from executing his duties as a Seventh Cavalry officer, regardless of who might be in command.

There is an interesting footnote to the Washita campaign. In March 1869, General Sheridan, having grown weary of the Cheyenne problem, once again set out to bring an end to the ways of the red race. Custer, determined to bring them in, be it by battle or by diplomacy, was to undergo an experience that would prove to be strangely prophetic.

Because the Indians were holding two white women captive, Custer thought diplomacy might be the safest way to handle the situation. As he and Lieutenant W. W. Cooke sat down in the lodge of the chief, Custer was placed beneath the "Medicine Arrows" (a very sacred symbol to the Cheyenne) and soon was sharing in the Indian custom of smoking the peace pipe. Also participating in the ceremony was the medicine man who, unknown to G.A.C., was spewing out Cheyenne promises of destruction should Custer attempt to use violence against their people. The medicine man proceeded to pour the ashes from the pipe bowl onto the same boots which conquered Black Kettle's Washita camp, the intent of which was to bring bad luck upon this continually lucky officer. Only time would tell.

Chapter Three

THE YEAR OF PREMONITIONS

The centennial year 1876 was to be a year of celebration for the United States of America. People everywhere were caught up in the preparations pertaining to the nation's one hundredth birthday. The deep wounds caused by the Civil War were beginning to heal as leaders from across the country pledged their mutual support. When the Mayor of Montgomery, Alabama, M. L. Moses, sent greetings to the centennial commission in Philadelphia, he was quick to remind them that while Montgomery was the birthplace of the Confederate government, the city council wanted to extend a "...cordial and fraternal greeting to all the people of the United States, with an earnest prayer for the perpetuation of concord and brotherly feeling throughout our land." [1] The language does seem a bit archaic by today's standards. Yet when one stops to consider that only one decade earlier the sons of Montgomery and the sons of Philadelphia were desperately trying to kill each other, the words take on a special significance.

In the city of Memphis, Tennessee, ex-Confederate and ex-Union artillerymen joined forces for the firing of thirteen cannons, signaling the beginning of festivities for this special July fourth.[2] This time, however, the booming of the guns would not be followed by the screams of the wounded and the destruction of property, something the South had had quite enough of. Even so, the sound of the firing must have caused some residents to shudder.

From New York to San Francisco, America was gearing up for the lavish affair. Philadelphia was the actual hub of activity, as dignitaries from around the world gathered for the huge party, which included an exposition filled with hundreds of exhibits featuring the latest technological wonders of western man. This was going to be a special summer and everyone knew it.

Yet not all Americans were sharing in the revelry, for the Native American had little to celebrate. But then, this was usually the case when confronted with the ever-growing power of the white world. They would have their own time of celebration, not in cities and towns like the white man, but out on the Great Plains. And it would be here, on a barren Montana field, that a series of events would culminate, and the summer of joy would quickly dissolve into the summer of violence. And 1876 would prove to be a drastic year of change for both of these cultures.

The actual campaign against the Sioux would involve several columns of troops in what was to be, more or less, a search-and-destroy mission. During the months of April and May, Colonel John Gibbon combed the wilds north of the Yellowstone, during which time some light contact was made with the Sioux. On June 16, General Crook's detachment marched north from their base camp, which was situated near the present-day town of Sheridan, Wyoming. General Alfred H. Terry, whose force consisted of several companies of infantry, as well as Custer's Seventh Cavalry, departed Fort Abraham Lincoln on May 17. By June 22, Terry would allow Custer's Seventh to break free from the main command to pursue the hostiles.

As always, spring marked the time when the Indians would flee the reservation provided them by the Great Father, choosing instead the wild and open country, for this was the place they had always called home. The government, however, having grown weary of Indian disobedience, was determined to solve this problem once and for all.

Although laws, treaties, and edicts are always comprised of words, their real strength lies in the steel and lead which must enforce those treaties. And so, it fell once again to the army to act as the instrument of enforcement against the hostile Plains Indians. If only the army could locate them before the elusive tactics of the Sioux again proved to be a problem. But the Indians had other ideas.

In mid-June, Sitting Bull held a sun dance, a ritual considered to be one of the most sacred of the Sioux. For several days the famous medicine man—now in middle age—subjected himself to the rigors and strains accompanying the dance, and on the third day received what he would later describe as a vision of soldiers falling headlong into camp. For Sitting Bull, this could only mean one thing: Any bluecoats foolish enough to attack his village would be utterly destroyed.

Had Custer had the opportunity to hear of Sitting Bull's vision before he reached the Little Bighorn, he no doubt would have laughed at such a statement, for he had always believed in the invincibility of his regiment, regardless of the size of the opposing force. Even so, he would have his own moments of doubt, as would many traveling with him. And herein lies one of the strangest aspects concerning this campaign. One the one hand is the confidence of the Sioux—a confidence which never falters, even with the arrival of the soldiers—and on the other is the despair and foreboding of the attackers and their families, that would prove to be all too prophetic.

When the Seventh Cavalry marched out of Ft. Abraham Lincoln on the morning of May 17, it marked the appearance of a strange, invisible cloud of despair which seemed to descend upon the doomed command, acting as a type of warning not to go. General Terry even used the occasion to bolster the spirits of the families by assembling the troops in parade formation, accompanied of course by the ever-present band sending forth another fighting tune. But just as Sitting Bull felt certain that his prediction of disaster for the U.S.

Army would come true, many who witnessed this particular send off also believed that disaster was on the horizon for the Seventh Cavalry.

Recalling the scene years later, Libbie Custer wrote: "Mothers, with strange eyes, held out their young ones...for one last look at their departing Fathers...the grief of these women was audible and was accompanied by desponding gestures..."[3]

Despite the disconcerting alarm among the women, 925 troops trotted out in a formal, two-abreast column, followed by supporting supply wagons and mule trains loaded with ammunition. Also traveling with the command were forty Indian scouts and several white scouts and interpreters, as well as a number of civilians, among them Custer's brother, Boston, and his nephew, "Autie" Reed.

Libbie, along with Custer's sister, Mrs. James Calhoun, was allowed to accompany the regiment on its first day's march. Early in the afternoon, camp was made on the bank of the Heart River. When the command marched away the following morning, Libbie recounts how an event occurred to enhance her fears. After breaking camp, while the sunlight began to penetrate the morning mist, a strange sight appeared that would again prove prophetic for the mighty Seventh. "Soon the bright sun began to penetrate this vail and dispel the haze....and a scene of wonder and beauty appeared...." This thing of beauty turned out to be a mirage in which the column appeared to rise from the earth and "...thenceforth for a little distance it marched equally plain to the sight on the earth and in the sky...."[4]

From this moment onward, Libbie's apprehension became more acute and would continue without letup. Even her usual activities provided no relief, and she, along with many others, would remain within this cloud of despair until the news of the disaster finally reached them. Of particular interest was the emotional state of the women on June 25, the afternoon of the battle. While their husbands were fighting for their lives, a number of the women gathered in the Custer home for the singing of hymns, but this also failed to provide the comfort that would drive away their inner fears. One women even collapsed onto the floor and buried her head into the lap of another. Describing the scene, Libbie wrote: "All were absorbed in the same thoughts, and their eyes were filled with far-away visions...." Only later would she learn that their fears were justified, for at that very hour "...the souls of those we thought upon were ascending to their Maker."[5]

Very often, when one is about to be killed in battle, a strange inner knowing, a premonition of sorts, develops whereby the doomed individual begins sensing that his or her death is imminent and will very often begin verbalizing this fact. War, of course, provides many such opportunities, and it is amazing just how accurate many of these unfortunate souls can be. [During the Second World War, my uncle was a member of a five-inch gun crew aboard the heavy cruiser *U.S.S. Astoria*. Having joined the Navy in the peaceful year of 1940 (peaceful for America, that is), he would find his world turned upside down the following year when the Japanese attacked Pearl Harbor. After seeing action during the battles of the Coral Sea and Midway, he participated in the August 7, 1942 landing of the Marines on the island of Guadalcanal. Yet, before going into this battle he had a strange feeling that he would be killed, a fact he expressed to his two best friends aboard ship. During the early morning hours of August 9, the Japanese struck the American Fleet, sinking three U.S. heavy cruisers—including the *Astoria*—as well as an Australian cruiser. True to his feeling, my uncle was killed, yet his two friends lived.]

Charley Reynolds, nicknamed "Lonesome Charley" had experienced similar strange feelings some sixty-six years earlier. Having been employed as a scout with the Seventh for a number of years, Reynolds was picked to accompany the expedition on the Little Bighorn adventure. But Reynolds was having some very bad feelings about the upcoming campaign. According to Fred Girard, an interpreter with the Seventh, Reynolds twice confided in him that he expected to die on the campaign. Girard advised him to go and see General Terry so that, being a civilian, he might be excused. But Girard said Terry "...shamed him out of it." [6] Reynolds would die shortly after the first shots of this battle began. Had he been a little more forceful with Terry, he would have been spared this untimely death.

As for Custer, there was no observable anxiety on his part as he said good-bye to his precious Libbie at the Heart River camp a day earlier. Yet the grief being expressed by the families at Ft. Abraham Lincoln must have had an effect on him, and his men as well. Even so, it would be just four days before his death that Custer would experience the same type of trepidation which engulfed those he bid farewell to at the start of this campaign.

On the 21st of June, the Seventh was camped at the mouth of Rosebud Creek. Here Custer, along with Terry and Colonel Gibbon, engaged in a conference aboard the steamer *Far West*—the same steamer which would, in just a very few days, carry the wounded and survivors away from the scene of disaster. During this time Custer would emerge a changed man, his former confidence replaced by an unspoken sense of doom. Indeed, this gloom seems to have floated over the entire command. Letters were written, and wills were made, remembers Lieutenant Godfrey who felt that his fellow officers must have had a "...presentiment of their fate." [7]

At noon on the 22nd, the Seventh broke camp and continued their march into destiny. Before their departure, Custer was offered the Second Cavalry which, true to his character, he flatly rejected. His reason for rejecting this additional firepower, he said, was that the Seventh Cavalry could handle anything it came up against. In Custer's mind, the regiment was both omnipotent and immortal. When he was offered the use of Gatling guns, his response was the same.

At 4 p.m., the regiment made camp. Custer was now twelve miles closer to battle. At dusk, officers call was sounded, and Custer began relating to his officers in a most unusual way. "This 'talk' of his," as Lieutenant Godfrey recalled, "was considered at the time something extraordinary for General Custer, for it was not his habit to unbosom himself to his officers. In it he showed a lack of self-confidence, a reliance on somebody else; there was a indefinable something that was not Custer." [8] This, of course, had a profound effect on those gathered around their leader, and such an odd expression of his personality no doubt proved to heighten their own fears as well. As Godfrey and Lieutenant Wallace were returning to their respective areas, Wallace blurted out: "Godfrey, I believe General Custer is going to be killed." When Godfrey asked him why he felt this way, Wallace responded, "Because I have never heard Custer talk in that way before." [9] The caution lights were certainly flashing now for the Seventh Cavalry, but without effect.

Unknown to Custer, the Army's three-pronged offensive to defeat the Sioux was now only two, as warriors had soundly whipped the forces under General Crook on the 17th of June. Led by the legendary Crazy Horse, Crook's troops were defeated in what is known as the Battle of the Rosebud, an area only a few miles south of where the Custer debacle would unfold. Ironically, the field in which Crook's battle was fought contains an ancient buffalo jump. Indeed, many of the jump sites around the Tongue and Powder Rivers in Montana and Wyoming date back several thousand years. This area had always been a good place to stalk their prey.[10] On this day, however, the Indians where hunting game of the two-legged variety, and it was the U.S. Army and not the buffalo they were intending to stampede. After the battle, Crook returned to his base camp, refusing to leave again until reinforcements could be added to his command. Later on Crook would make the absurd claim that his forces hadn't suffered a defeat at the Rosebud, but this claim is completely without foundation as the facts clearly show otherwise.

And while Custer would die without the knowledge of Crook's defeat—a defeat that could have acted as a warning—he did have plenty of voices surrounding him that were both knowledgeable of the enemy's strength and were constantly warning him of the dangers which lay ahead.

Mitch Boyer, the famous half-breed scout (his father was French, his mother a full-blooded Sioux) had been loaned to Custer by Colonel Gibbon and would ultimately perish with the doomed command. With some thirty years' experience on the Plains, Custer should have weighed carefully the advice given him by Boyer concerning the number of the Sioux they would have to fight, for his assessment was exactly the same as that of Custer's own trusted scout, Bloody Knife. Indeed, on the last morning of their lives, Bloody Knife told Custer that there were more Sioux than the soldiers had bullets, but nothing could deter Custer's imagined triumph over the hostiles, and all such warnings bounced off of Custer like bullets ricocheting off of a stone wall. How tragic it must have been for those who knew such blind disregard was likely going to result in their own deaths. Yet this was the case for all of those who followed Custer into the valley of the Little Bighorn on that hot and dusty Sabbath.

Custer's failure to heed the advice of his scouts may be due in part to a strong feeling that white interpretation of facts, militarily speaking, was always superior to that of the Indians'. A case in point would be Custer's failure to believe the Osage scout after he detected the odor of fire just before the attack on Black Kettle's camp. Only when the remains of a fire were discovered did the white hunters believe him. Custer would learn the accuracy of his scouts at Little Bighorn as well, but by the time this was discovered it would be too late. Unlike Custer, they were not West Point-trained, but they could—and did—run circles around the majority of West Pointers when it came to scouting. This is why the Army always employed Indians for the tracking of other Indians. Captain Benteen, who had seen on occasion how accurately they could ply their trade, felt Custer's refusal to heed their warnings was foolish indeed.

When Custer asked Fred Girard his opinion concerning the number of hostiles they likely would encounter, Girard responded not less than twenty-five hundred,[11] an estimate fully one thousand more than Custer expected to meet. Having sought out the advice of Girard, one might be inclined to think that Girard's higher figure would have sparked the necessary caution within Custer, slowing him down somewhat, giving him the time to take a second look at the situation. Yet none of this would occur.

At 5 a.m. on the morning of the 23rd, the command was on the move, marching up the Rosebud. Because of the slow-moving pack train, the regiment was obliged to halt after a trek of only fifteen miles. Signs of large Indian movements were everywhere, and before the day's march was completed they would pass the remains of three different hostile camps, each ranging in diameter between one-third to one-half mile wide. Still, the boy-general could not perceive the dangers which lay like coiled snakes just ahead, and it must have appeared to the Indians, who were aware of their presence, that Sitting Bull's vision of the Army's destruction would indeed come to pass.

The several-hundred-yard-wide trail which the troops followed on the 23rd was enlarged by the 24th to one-half mile wide and was very fresh.[12] The ground the Seventh was crossing was quite rough in spots, the bluffs being broken, which caused the regiment to follow a meandering course in their trek in the valley.[13] By day's end the command had covered approximately thirty-three miles.

The march of the 24th brought Custer to an abandoned camp much larger than the previous ones encountered. At this camp, however, stood a "Sun Dance" Lodge which contained the scalp of a white man, no doubt one of Colonel Gibbon's men killed several weeks earlier. Here Custer gathered his officers together to discuss the situation. It was at this time, as the group gathered, that a strange and, to some, disturbing incident occurred, which was viewed as a bad omen for the Seventh Cavalry. "At this time a stiff southerly breeze was blowing," recalled Lieutenant Godfrey, "As we were about to separate, the General's head-quarters flag was blown down, falling to our rear. Being near the flag I picked it up and stuck the staff in the ground, but it fell again to the rear." [14]

The scouts, who had been quite thorough in their search, were paying special attention to the area around Tulloch's Creek. By day's end the command had marched some twenty-eight miles, finally making camp about sundown behind the cover of a bluff.

The troops, both tired and saddle-weary, would not be permitted to rest long. By 11:30 p.m., the Seventh was again in pursuit of their enemy and would not rest again until 2:30 a.m. By 3 a.m. the men were allowed to make coffee, but even this simple pleasure was spoiled as the water was filled with alkaline. "We almost gagged on it." remembered Private Charles Windolph of H company.[15]

By 2:30 a.m., Leiutenant Charles Varnum and his scouts had reached the place called the Crow's Nest. This is where the command would catch their first view of the great Sioux encampment. Within hours the regiment would again sound "Boots and Saddles" but for many it would be the last time.

Even though it was Custer's intention to draw as close to the Sioux as possible—all the while remaining undetected—and attack on the 26th as planned, circumstances would dictate otherwise. The time for premonitions was almost over, for the reality of the situation, like a brilliant flash, was about to engulf all the players in this sad drama. And in a very real sense, the light of the Seventh Cavalry was going out. Certainly after this day it would never be the same.

Chapter Four

VALLEY OF FEAR

A little before 8 a.m. on the last morning of his life, General George Armstrong Custer was summoned to the Crow's Nest to see for himself the hostile camp which awaited him. Not even waiting to saddle his horse, Custer rode bare- back throughout the camp spouting out orders to the various officers in charge. Custer was dressed in a blue-grey flannel shirt, buckskin trousers, and long cavalry boots. Although his hair was already short, as can be seen from his April, 1876, photograph, Custer trimmed his hair even shorter for this campaign. On this particular morning he was seen wearing a regular company hat.[1]

By 8:30 a.m. the Seventh was again up and moving, and the gloom which had been so prevalent with the troops was now ebbing away. In fact, many of the men were now joking with one another and feeling more confident than they had in days.[2]

After a very short march, lasting little more than an hour, the regiment halted and the troops concealed themselves in a ravine. But Custer, not willing to waste precious time, rode off towards the Crow's Nest where he could personally view his prize. Here again, Custer was warned just how vast a camp they were about to do battle with, but because he couldn't detect anything himself, even with field glasses, he did not believe the Indians were actually there. Perhaps this was due to Custer's viewing of the camp later in the morning when the sun was overhead, and the heat of the day, producing a haze, could easily have distorted the images before him.[3] Whatever it was, he refused to believe they were there, and only the Sioux and Cheyenne would benefit from his "blindness." Captain Benteen however, did believe it, saying, "...I'd sooner trust the sharp eye of an Indian than to trust a pretty good binocular..."[4]

Bloody Knife, destined to die along with his leader, gave Custer one final warning, begging him to use extreme caution, but this, too, was ignored by the boy-general who by now was little more than a Pied Piper leading his troops to an early grave. After additional information was brought to him which pointed to their discovery by the hostiles (or so he thought), he ordered his bugler to sound out "officers call." When the shrill sound of the bugle pierced the air, the entire command realized something was afoot as no bugle calls had been allowed during the previous two days' marches. The bugler, an Italian immigrant-turned soldier by the name of Giovanni Martini, stated that the officers came to Custer in a hurry and that the enlisted men were kept away.[5]

Having been discovered, Custer decided to attack at once, and as we shall see, this decision would not necessarily prove fatal, but it would mean that the Seventh Cavalry, greatly outnumbered, would be forced to fight without the assistance of the Gibbon and Terry forces. Unknown to Custer, but soon to be realized, was the actual size of the camp which lay sprawled in the valley of the Little Bighorn. Even so, it would be the accumulation of bad decisions which would dig the grave, so to speak, for the Seventh Cavalry.

As the regiment passed into the valley of the Little Bighorn, they were passing the point of no return. History was being made, and at a very high cost. It is certain that many following Custer on that hot day, especially the newer recruits, were convinced that the boy-general, who had led them into this wilderness, would also lead them out again. After all, this always followed Custer's spectacular charges into battle. To many, Custer and victory were one and the same. But the Indians, wanting only to be left alone, would not be so forgiving of those who brought fire and lead to their loved ones' doorsteps.

The camp which Custer thought would flee at the first sign of trouble was, by some estimates, the largest Indian gathering to ever occur on the North American Plains, and was between two and three miles in length. Highly organized, the various tribes camped in order, always retaining the same position relative to each other after every move. It was, so to speak, the Indian version of a city on wheels.

Occupying the lower end of the village were the Hunkpapa Sioux. These would be the first to encounter Major Reno's charge into the valley. Next were the Sans-arc followed by the Minneconjou, Blackfoot Sioux, Santee Sioux, Yankton, Oglala (from which Crazy Horse would spring), and the Brule. Comprising the northern end of the camp were the famous fighters, the Cheyenne. It would be here, at the Cheyenne camp, that Custer would appropriately present himself like a lamb to the slaughter. Did he remember the 1869 Cheyenne promise of death should he ever attack the Cheyenne again? Of this we can only speculate, for any white man unfortunate enough to survey the scene did not live to tell of it. The Cheyenne, of course, were more than willing to keep their promise, and the Sioux were very eager to help them.

At approximately 12:20 p.m., Custer made the fatal decision to split his command. By doing so, he ensured his own defeat. As he was under the impression that his presence had been discovered, he fully expected the enemy to flee. This was his worst fear, for he knew just how adept they were in their ability to quickly break camp and disappear over the horizon. This is why the Army was constantly forced to employ Indians in the pursuit of other Indians.

The first to be dispatched was Captain Benteen. Earlier in the day when Custer, Benteen, Charley Reynolds and several other officers were gathered together, Private Charles

Windolph overheard Reynolds warning them concerning the size of the camp they were about to attack. During the conversation he heard Captain Benteen say to Custer, "Hadn't we keep the regiment together, General? If this is as big of a camp as they say, we'll need every man we have." But Custer, whose mind was now closed like a steel trap, and whose destruction was completely assured, could only utter, "You have your orders."[6] Benteen knew the order was foolish before the last word had fallen from the General's lips. But orders were orders. As he would later testify, his orders were "...to precede out into a line of bluffs about four or five miles away, to pitch into anything I came across and to send back word..."[7] After traveling about one mile, a messenger was dispatched informing Benteen that if nothing was discovered he was to continue his march to the second line of bluffs. After another mile, a sergeant major caught up with him, informing him of Custer's wish that if he still had seen no sign of the enemy after the second line of bluffs, he was to continue into the valley, and if still nothing had been found, he was to proceed into the next valley.[8]

In Benteen's mind, his trek to the left would take his command away from the main body at a forty-five degree angle to only God knew where. Under Benteen's immediate command were companies H, D, and K. Later on, he would describe the ground over which they marched as "...very rugged."[9] Windolph said the hills they were forced to cross were "...pitching and bucking as far as you could see."[10]

Soon after this, Custer ordered Major Reno to take companies A, G, and M. This left Custer with companies C, E, F, I, and L under his direct command. Captain McDougall, in charge of the slow-moving, but terribly vital pack train, would meander into the chaos later that afternoon.

Although separated, the Reno-Custer columns would travel together for some distance. When they arrived at the spot known as the Lone Tepee, which contained the remains of a warrior who had been killed in the fight with Crook, events began to quicken. From this point, the two commands would separate forever. Fred Girard, who had advanced to a nearby hill some forty or fifty yards from the dead Indian's lodge, was able to see a part of the village as well as a pony herd. "Then I hollered to General Custer, `Here are your Indians, running like devils.'" [11] A number of Indians were seen to be fleeing towards the Little Bighorn, and because the Ree scouts would not pursue the fleeing warriors, Custer ordered Reno to take up the chase. Several miles in the distance lay Custer's prize, and already dust could be seen rising from the southern tip of the village as Sitting Bull's people made preparations for their safety.

Reno's orders, which were sent to him through Custer's adjutant, W.W. Cooke, were quite clear: He was to cross the river, attack the hostiles, while Custer would support him with the whole command. This promise of direct support was taken literally by Reno and by the other officers as well. Once the first shots were fired, they fully expected Custer to come sweeping down into the valley and through this combined effort destroy the Sioux. When this didn't happen, another sequence of events, a mini debacle, if you will, began to unfold, unraveling the Seventh in a most humiliating way.

Meanwhile, Benteen was moving at a "left oblique" over ground no sane Indian would travel, and McDougall, carrying the most important element for any battle—the ammunition—would soon be so far in the rear that his ability to supply the command in time would be severely limited.

Soon the galloping command would reach the bank of the Little Bighorn River, where it would then cross into the valley and into the jaws of the Sioux. Before crossing however, the column all but halted so as to allow the extremely thirsty horses to drink from the cool stream. A number of the troops wisely chose to fill their canteens as well before moving out into the valley.

Before Reno completed his task of getting his troops across the river, which at that point did not exceed twenty-five feet in width, the scouts shouted a warning that the Sioux were coming to meet them. When Reno heard this, he dispatched a messenger to Custer informing him of the situation. By doing so, Reno sealed the poor sergeant's fate, as he was never heard from again. The interpreter, Girard, sent a warning as well, telling William Cooke and Captain Myles Keogh, both of whom had been riding with the Reno contingent towards the battle.

By the time Cooke and Keogh reached Custer, he had stopped to water the horses at the stream known today as Reno Creek. And while we know that this word of warning reached Custer, the promise of direct support would not be forthcoming. Now disintegration would tear at Reno's three companies, and total annihilation awaited those racing ahead with Custer.

After crossing the river, Reno led his troops down the valley. Custer, having turned in a northerly direction, rode along the bluffs and would have been able to see Reno as he approached his moment of battle. Here, too, Custer would gain his first real view—albeit a partial one—of the hostile village. Of course, had it been his intention to support Reno as he engaged the Indians, now would have been the time to do so. Yet given his mode of thinking, and how he desired to alter battle plans according to what he saw going on around him, it is not at all surprising that he did not return. Not only was this decision going to prove disastrous, but his failure to include his staff in whatever battle plans he intended to execute, would be nothing short of suicidal. Benteen, ever critical of Custer's tactics, later testified that he believed Custer had no plan, and that if he did, he kept it to himself. [12]

It was approximately 2:30 p.m. when Reno's troops charged down the valley of the Little Bighorn. At about this same time Benteen decided that if he was going to be of any assistance to the command he would need to join them as quickly as possible. He felt—quite correctly—that his jaunt to the left was a useless adventure, and that only his decision to disobey orders now would put him in a position to help the command once contact with the hostiles was actually made.

Little did the captain realize that this "disobedience" would result in the salvation of Reno's bloodied command.

First Sergeant John M. Ryan, of company M, remembered well the charge onto the wide and open valley on that hot Sunday afternoon. He recalled that while they were galloping, Lieutenant Charles Varnum called out, "Thirty days furlough to the man who gets the first scalp." [13] Although Ryan was eager for a furlough, he said he didn't share Varnum's enthusiasm for such a trophy. Given the fact that Varnum had seen a portion of the Indian village just a short time earlier, and had come to the conclusion that the camp contained an "...immence number of Indians...more than I ever saw before..." [14] one has to wonder whether his statement concerning the scalp contained more gallows humor than sincerity.

Meanwhile, the Sioux took action to save their people. Riding their ponies back and forth, the warriors created clouds of dust which served as a smoke screen while the women, children, and old men had time to escape. Years later, Chief Gall, of the Hunkpapa tribe, remembered how rapidly Reno swept down into the valley, forcing the warriors into a premature fight.[15] Of course, Reno's trek into the valley put him on a collision course with the large hostile camp. Besides the dust billowing up before them, which served the Indians well, the warriors had also started a number of fires on the dry prairie. Up until now, the Souix had kept themselves just out of rifle range as they acted as a buffer between the camp and the soldiers. Yet this charge, which was destined to become an important part in the legacy of Marcus A. Reno, came skidding to an abrupt halt. From this moment on, confusion would reign within the ranks of the Seventh Cavalry.

Although the valley appeared flat, with the Little Bighorn river snaking its way on the troopers' right, and foothills off to their left, Reno testified that he saw a ditch containing a large number of Indians, which came pouring out onto the plain; a fact that was confirmed by several other officers, including Lieutenant Wallace.

Reno aborted the charge at a place where the river looped out leftward onto the prairie. Directly in front of this loop was a timber of young cottonwood trees that contained a glade, or swale, in it's center. Just as the troopers approached this timber some of the men discharged their weapons into the woods in the hope that any Indians hiding there would be encouraged to leave.[16] Two unfortunate souls who were unable to control their horses continued galloping towards the village and were swallowed up by the enraged Sioux. As the skirmish line was formed, the right end of the line reached the timber and continued leftward out toward the foothills. This is where the scouts George Herendeen and Charlie Reynolds, along with the interpreter, Girard, positioned themselves to keep out of the soldiers' way.

The Sioux, whose actions up until now had remained defensive, would soon press the attack, and Reno would not have to wait very long. Having dismounted, the troops began a concentrated fire at the Indians, who were still some five to eight hundred yards away. Although the firing at this distance was not accurate, the forty-five-caliber carbine rounds did begin falling into the camp, clipping leaves off of trees, puncturing tepees, and wounding and killing a number of the Sioux who were running about.

During a July 1886 interview, which appeared in the *St. Paul Pioneer Press*, Chief Gall related how he was transformed through his own personal loss as Reno's skirmish line fired into the village: "My two squaws and three children were killed there...and it made my heart bad. After that I killed all my enemies with the hatchet." [17] According to Sergeant Ryan, the first cavalryman to fall dead on the line was Miles F. Ohara of Company M. Ohara, only days before a corporal, had been promoted to sergeant, replacing a Sergeant Dolan whose military career—but not his life—was about to expire. Dolan missed the battle as he was allowed to remain at the base camp at Powder River.

Many of the troops were very green and inexperienced, and were firing their weapons rapidly, despite the protests of the officers. Testifying later, Myles Moylan said that it was "...impossible for an officer to regulate it, owing to the men being new in the service, and not under fire before." [18] Sergeant Edward Davern, who was situated to the left of the line, and had crawled about two hundred yards ahead of the firing line to shoot at some Indians another two hundred yards farther out, also took notice of this rapid firing. Still situated to the left of the line were the scouts Herendeen, Reynolds, and Girard. As they sat there watching the troops hurling lead at the distant village, they decided to set the sights of their rifles on one Indian in particular. The distance however was too great, and as Herendeen remembered, "We could see all the balls fall short of the Indian...." He added that this was the only firing they did while on the prairie.[19]

It must be noted that later testimony by the officers varied somewhat regarding the number of Indians they were facing. However, it does seem certain that within minutes of the skirmish line being formed there were several hundred yelping warriors facing them, and that their numbers were gaining strength by the minute. Lieutenant Wallace must have felt they were quite strong as he later testified that the Indians "...were ready to receive us."[20] Anyway, it wasn't long before the soldiers' entire front was blanketed with warriors who were doing an excellent job of flanking the troops and forcing the left wing to give ground. Although the line endeavored to maintain its position, the left end was forced to bend back and soon would be parallel to the river. At about this same time, Reno led Company G through the timber to a spot where a few Indian lodges from the southernmost tip of the camp nearly touched the woods. Evidently he was concerned about hostile infiltration from that direction and was attempting to avert any problems that would come from a breach in his line. While a breach in his line was not yet a reality, a breach in his mind was about to occur.

As Reno made his way through the woods with G Company, he was fully aware of the deteriorating situation of the skirmish line, and it only stands to reason that Custer's "no show" was playing on his mind as well. According to Lieutenant Wallace, twenty of those following Reno were brand-new recruits to G Company, having been picked up by the regiment in April in St. Paul, Minnesota. One can easily imagine their state of mind as they, unfamiliar carbines in hand, followed Reno through the woods to God knew where, all the while silent regrets poured out of them as forcefully as the sweat that was now drenching their clothes.

Meanwhile, the warriors were vigorously pressing the attack and the withdrawal of G Company from the line for Reno's trek through the timber did not help matters at all. Unable to hold their line any longer, the troops headed for the woods. Lieutenant Varnum said that while the timber was quite thick, there were paths leading into it made by the various animals inhabiting the area. Even so, their time spent in the woods would be very short. Indeed, the confusion which drove the troops from the prairie only followed them into the trees. The blue-coated hunters had now become the blue-coated hunted. The warriors, spurred on by their successful intimidation of the soldiers, now swirled around the timber, shouting and firing into it at will. For some of the troops, being driven into the woods did have its advantages as a number of them were out of ammunition and could now get to their horses to retrieve more.

As can be expected, the Indians were becoming more bold in their actions, breaching the lines in several places and soon a steady rain of bullets were buzzing in on the men. As Reno discused the situation with several officers, he came to the conclusion that the command should make a run for the hills on the other side of the Little Bighorn. Although Reno almost immediately began calling this action a "charge," he did refer to it as a "retreat" when discussing the situation with Captain Moylan.[22] And just as his decision to abort his charge in the valley would later be grounds for rebuke, what occurred next would haunt the major all the days of his life.

As Reno conferred with the scout Bloody Knife concerning the possible intention of the hostiles, the Sioux unleashed a stream of lead which killed Bloody-Knife as well as a Private Lorentz. Bloody Knife, who had been standing only several feet from Reno, was hit in the head, the impact of which showered the Major with the brains and blood of the dead scout. During the Civil War, Reno had seen plenty of head wounds, and blood spewing like geysers from the bodies of those mortally wounded was certainly nothing new to him. Still, this incident does appear to be the proverbial straw which broke the camel's back. Having succumbed to some degree of terror, the major bolted from the timber, followed by those lucky enough to have heard the order to retreat. Before leaving the woods however, Reno was so completely flustered by the killing of Bloody Knife and Private Lorentz, that he ordered those around him to dismount, but just as quickly he changed his mind and ordered them to mount up again. Thoughts of disaster must have been racing through his mind faster than the bullets that were zipping around him. Within seconds, Reno was bounding out of the woods.

As commanding officer, Reno could have banished such confusion among his troops by employing the proper bugle calls, and should have done so. The sound of bugles would certainly have stood out among the shrieks of the Indians, the cursing of the troops, and the blasts of rifles, which by now had become quite steady. Given the facts of this exodus, it is very difficult to view Reno's flight from the woods as anything but an attempt at self-preservation. Herendeen believed the killing of Bloody Knife startled everyone and was to blame for the quick departure. At about the same time as this was occurring, Lieutenant Varnum began to notice that "...a great many bullets had commenced to drop into the woods from our rear...I could here the bullets chip the trees as they would strike." [23]

Lieutenant Hare, who later testified that he was unaware that an order to leave the timber had been given, said that he first learned of the move when Private Clare of K Company brought him his horse. Had it not been for private Clare, Hare believed, he might have been left to his fate in the woods. Sadly, Clare, whose hands brought deliverance to Hare, would not be counted among the survivors at battle's end.

Dr. Henry Porter, the only physician of three to survive the expedition, remembered hearing someone saying "...we had to get out of here, that we had to charge the Indians..." [24] But the good doctor was of the opinion that instead of the troops charging the Indians, it appeared the Indians were "...driving the troops." He added that "Every man seemed to be running on his own hook." Girard said the troops were in a great hurry to get out and that "there seemed to be no order at all. Every man was for himself." [25] As they rode off, Girard said he heard an officer shout out, "For God's sake men—

don't leave—we have wounded...."[26] Herendeen later would identify this officer as Lieutenant Charles Varnum, but Varnum's cries went unheeded.

The distance between the timber and where the command would cross the Little Bighorn River (actually, the command was forced to retreat in a southeasterly direction), was a little over one-half of a mile away, and the Indians, already surrounding the command in great numbers, were determined to spill as much Seventh Cavalry blood as possible.

As Reno led the command across the prairie towards the river, the fighting was desperate, and as Sergeant Ryan remembers: "As we cut through them the fighting was hand to hand, and it was death to any man who fell from his horse..."[27] Many Indians were content galloping alongside of the soldiers, picking them off with a steady fire from their weapons. Lieutenant Varnum recalled how the Indians would "...sit there and work their rifles."[28] For these warriors it must have seemed more like a buffalo hunt than a contest of equals. The troops, however, who offered absolutely no organized response to this enfilading fire, would suffer heavy casualties in what can only be considered as a gauntlet-like retreat.

Unknown to Reno's men, a number of the Sioux chasing them were not just shouting their war cries, but were chiding them because they had whipped them along the Rosebud—an obvious reference to General Crook's defeat eight days earlier.[29]

As the troops plunged their horses down the embankment and into the water, Reno paused to survey the scene. The rear of the column was now swirling in confusion as the Indians kept up a steady fire into what Reno could only describe as "...a very large target." [30] Dr. Porter remembered that he had quite a bit of difficulty mounting his horse when it came time to leave the woods. After dashing through a number of warriors who were between him and the command, as well as a large number who were to his right firing into the troops, he neared the river bank, and like Reno could see that the rear of the command was "...in no order at all. Every man seemed to be running on his own hook." [31] He could also see a number of mounted Indians on the opposite bank of the river firing at a dozen or so troops who were now in the water. At no time did he see any officer attempting to stabilize the situation, adding that he saw no officers at all until he himself had crossed the river.

At least one officer did attempt to stem the tide of confusion. The scout Herendeen, who later said the troops were running for their lives, remembered one officer shouting "Company A men halt...let us fight them, for God's sake don't run." [32] This officer was probably Lieutenant Varnum as well.

The hilltop that the troops were trying so desperately to reach was extremely steep and was accessible by the various jagged ravines and gullies which led up to the top of the hill. Unfortunately, some of these ravines were accessible to the Indians as well, either in person or well within the sights of their guns. Dr. Dewolf, having survived the perilous flight from the timber, was cut down in one of these gullies by Indians who were firing down from the hilltop. Varnum, following behind Dewolf, was warned just in time by the shouts of the others who had seen the hostiles positioning themselves, thereby escaping the same fate as that of the fallen doctor. Many of the men led their horses up these ravines, although a number of troops remained mounted the entire time. Indeed, a number of the wounded made it all the way up to the top before falling off their mounts. Evidently, one trooper decided to take Varnum at his word, for he was seen ascending the hill with the scalp of a Sioux clutched in his hand.

In terms of casualties, the race from the timber had been quite costly: forty dead, with more than a half dozen wounded. True to his inner feelings, the scout Reynolds was among the dead who fell in the valley fight. Witnesses said the Indians shot his horse out from under him, which feel on him, pinning him under its weight. After the fight, those who had the opportunity of reclaiming the dead said he had put up a good fight as a number of empty cartridge casings were scattered about him.

It was between 3:30 and 4 p.m., and Benteen's troop was now approaching the scene of Reno's fiasco. After crossing the Little Bighorn, Benteen followed Custer's route and headed up the bluffs, for he had seen Reno's men being driven from the skirmish line and into the timber. At this time Benteen was not aware that the confused fight did not include the entire command. Benteen's arrival on the hilltop, as well as the arrival of the pack train about an hour later, would be a critical factor in the salvation of Reno's shaken band. Salvation for Custer however, was now beyond the realm of possibility, as events were unfolding very quickly, and nothing would avert Custer from obtaining a great victory over the Sioux.

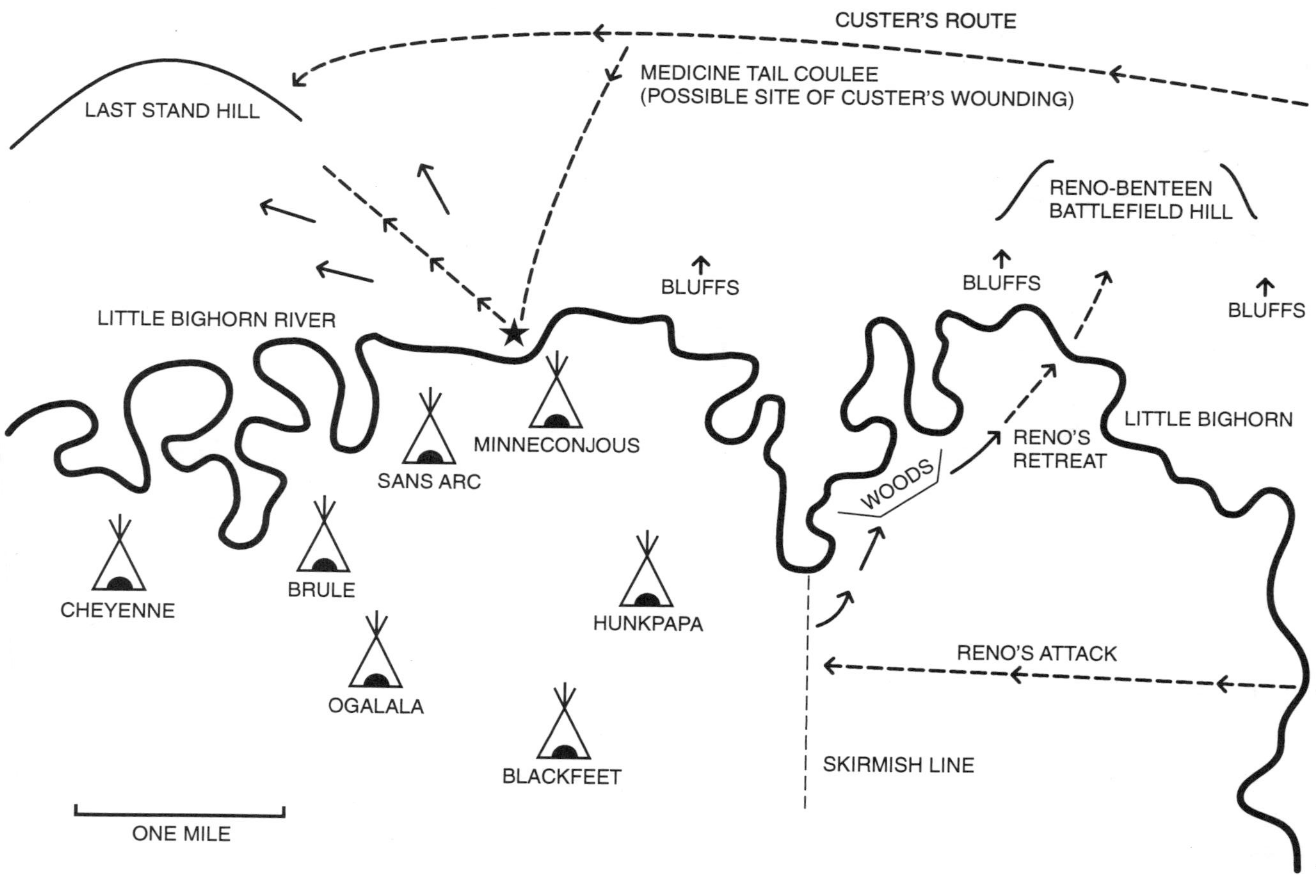
CUSTER'S ROUTE
MEDICINE TAIL COULEE
(POSSIBLE SITE OF CUSTER'S WOUNDING)
LAST STAND HILL
RENO-BENTEEN
BATTLEFIELD HILL
BLUFFS
BLUFFS
BLUFFS
LITTLE BIGHORN RIVER
LITTLE BIGHORN
MINNECONJOUS
SANS ARC
CHEYENNE
BRULE
OGALALA
HUNKPAPA
BLACKFEET
WOODS
RENO'S
RETREAT
RENO'S ATTACK
SKIRMISH LINE
ONE MILE

June 25, 1876

Chapter Five

FIELD OF DEATH

After watching the opening round of Reno's attack, Custer rode on with his five companies over the high ground, never to be seen alive again. Yet even having the advantage of being in an elevated position, he was yet to learn the true size of this militant Indian encampment. The horses, already suffering exhaustion from the pace of the preceding days, labored heavily under this gallop of death. In Custer's mind however, everything was falling into place. The final blow against the Plains Indians was about to be struck, and Custer was happy to be playing a very important part in their defeat. Or so he thought.

As they raced northward, an even clearer view of the camp appeared, and it was evidently here that Custer dispatched his first messenger to the rear to gather the command that he himself had dispersed. That messenger was Sergeant Daniel Kanipe of Company M. Years after the battle, Kanipe related how he and Sergeant Finkle had been riding very close to Captain Tom Custer when Finkle's horse began to wear out. This would prove to be Finkle's undoing, as Kanipe believed that Finkle would have been given the duty of messenger had his horse not succumbed to exhaustion. In any event, Tom Custer ordered Kanipe to ride back to the pack train and give them the message to hurry along the high ground for there was a big village down below.[1] Kanipe said that as they approached the camp the men began to cheer, such was their joy over the enemy they were about to defeat. Today, however, if you travel to Little Bighorn Battlefield National Monument, you can read the names of those cheering troopers on the monument which sits atop their common grave on Last Stand Hill. Sadly, two days after Finkle and Kanipe separated, Kanipe would view the dead body of his friend, and he would never forget that he owed his deliverance to his friend's worn out horse.

As Kanipe was dispatched, Custer's force traveled down a narrow ravine that would, after one mile, lead into a coulee known as Medicine Tail. At about the same time, Custer decided to send a second courier to the rear. Was the wonder warrior beginning to have second thoughts? Perhaps. Having ridden dangerously ahead of the pack train, as well as having sent Benteen on what he now knew was a useless adventure, was no doubt poking at his mind. Even so, he could have acknowledged his apprehension at this point, deciding to gallop back the same way he had come, regroup and then attack the camp. But this was not to be. In the midst of whatever concern that he experienced, he would ride on and conquer as he always had. This was the Custer way of making war.

Custer called out to trumpeter Martini, ordering him to ride back to Benteen with instructions to hurry up the pack train. As Martini was about to leave, he was stopped by Lieutenant W.W. Cooke, who hurriedly scribbled out a message:

> Benteen.
> Come on. Big Village.
> Be quick. Bring packs.
> W.W. Cooke.
> P.S. Bring pack. [sic]

Ripping the paper from his book, Cooke handed the message to the last white man to ever see Custer's command alive.

As Martini rode away with the hastily scribbled message, he heard gunfire. As he looked back, he could see the Indians firing into the command, some of them waving blankets hoping to frighten the soldiers' horses. After traveling a short distance, Martini came upon Boston Custer who had been riding hard to catch up with his brother. "Boz," as he was affectionately called, had been hired by the Seventh Cavalry to act as a forager. Although a civilian, this would not keep him from dying with his famous military brothers. "He was riding at a run," remembered Martini, "but when he saw me he checked his horse and shouted 'Where's the General?' and

I answered...'right behind the next ridge you'll find him.'" [2] And he did.

As Martini rode back over the same trail the command had just covered, he saw Reno's troops in action on the skirmish line which had already begun to give ground under Sioux pressure. Just then a number of hostiles spotted the trumpeter as he rode atop the bluffs and began firing at him. Although Martini was not struck, he would remain unaware that his horse had been hit until Benteen later pointed out the blood which was streaming out of the beast.

Benteen, after disobeying Custer's orders to continue on, finally linked up with the main trail just a short distance from the Lone Warrior tepee, which was now burning. According to Benteen, it was here that Custer's first messenger came into view. Sergeant Kanipe quickly relayed the message that he had received from Captain Tom Custer to "Hurry up the packs." [3] Benteen sent him on to the pack train which was now, unknown to Benteen, only one mile in the rear. Accompanied by his orderly, Benteen rode on four or five hundred yards in advance of the battalion. When he encountered Martini and read the note, he ordered the command to proceed at a trot. Galloping ahead, he reached the Little Bighorn before the rest of the command and could see Reno's men being "thrashed" in the valley, but he was at the time unaware that it was only Reno's men and not the entire command. Martini had assured Benteen that the Indians were "skedaddling" but "...my first sight of the fight showed that there was no skedaddling being done." [4]

Within minutes Benteen's troops were charging up the bluffs, pistols drawn, fully expecting to meet the Sioux once the top was reached. But instead of painted faces and feathered heads, they found the hilltop beginning to swarm with Reno's beaten remnant. It was now approximately 4 p.m.

But where was Custer?

It is important to add here that from the moment that trumpeter Martini left Custer carrying that famous last message, it is impossible to ascertain what exactly occurred with the Custer command. Indian testimony varies and is sometimes conflicting in nature, and because no white man lived to tell the tale, interpreting the exact sequence of events is difficult indeed. Now that all participants are long dead, certain events shall remain eternally shrouded in mystery. Even so, archaeology—that "voice" from the ground—has unearthed some interesting facts concerning this battle. Yet even the slow, methodical hand of the archaeologist cannot tell us everything.

A word about Indian testimony is important here as well. Unlike the soldiers, who are ordered into battle by their officers and must remain with their own units, the Indian is free to choose his own course of actions in battle. If he desires to be a part of a particular group, then he will be a part of that group. If not, he's free to fight as he wishes. For example, when Crazy Horse became aware of Reno's valley attack he shouted out for the brave ones to follow him while ordering cowards to the rear. Of course, a man like Crazy Horse inspired those around him by his own actions, as did other Indians who were recognized as leaders. Although warriors did move as units, the participants did so willingly and were free to leave and scurry about the battlefield as they saw fit. During the Custer fight, warriors joined the fight at different times and at various places, and as the tide of battle carried people over the hills and gullies which are so plentiful in this area of the country, each warrior would later carry his own mental picture of how events unfolded. This is quite natural, and confusion concerning certain aspects can occur.

In addition, it must be remembered that all Indian testimony came after—sometimes years after—the fight occurred and the speaker was now a "conquered" Indian living in a dominant white culture. As such, the Indians may have been more likely to relay certain events in a manner that would please their white audience than to tell the truth. After all, some of these veterans took on almost celebrity status and became very adept at raking in the white man's coin. Why should they depress their audience by telling them the truth when they could sugarcoat it, keep them happy, and make a living for themselves as well. Such is the universal nature of the human race which is not likely to change.

Anyway, after dispatching Martini, Custer rode down Medicine Tail Coulee, but just how far is open to debate even today. It is certain that at least two companies did reach the river's edge, as artifacts such as shell casings have been found at this spot.[5] This agrees with various Indian testimony which said the soldiers came to the river's edge and fired across the river at the camp. These troops, comprising the left wing, would soon move northward and away from the river in their attempt to rejoin the main command, which had been deployed on the high ground known today as the Nye-Cartwright Ridge. Although it is now a point of controversy, Custer probably did not encounter a horde of Indians here, although there were targets to shoot at. Even so, their numbers did grow rapidly, and Chief Gall would soon cross the river and began pressing the troops who were now falling back. By this time, Custer's five companies were well on their way to their final destination. Although the command was still functioning as an organized unit, it would not be long before small pockets of disintegration would appear as the Seventh Cavalry moved across the valleys and hills like a snake seeking refuge.

After Reno's men reached the hilltop they noticed that many of the Indians began racing back downstream and through their village. This movement would give Reno's shattered band time to recover and prepare a defense, but this release of warriors only added to Custer's problems. As the full force of Indians began to concentrate their efforts on Custer's five companies, they would employ a tactic of infiltration which would prove very effective. The ground over which the command was forced to travel is marked by hills, gullies, and ravines, and as the battle developed the troops began to fall over a wide area of this rough ground.

At what point Custer began to see his situation as serious remains a mystery. But there is no question that, as the strength of the hostiles became apparent, and the reinforcements from Benteen and Reno did not arrive, the question of survival must have become very real to him. Did he at this time remember the warning of his scouts? Although we will never know, it seems likely. What we do know is that as the blue-coated hunters swarmed up and down the various hills and ravines, they exchanged gunfire with the Sioux and Cheyenne warriors, most of whom where wisely fighting on foot, using the ground to their advantage. Although this infiltration would take some time, and would consist of Indian movements both north of Custer and south of the command, once the battle began in earnest, the death of the five companies would come very quickly. The Indians had not had it as good—or as easy—since the fight with the arrogant Captain Fetterman on that frigid December day ten years earlier. Today, however, the blue-coats were fighting under a blistering sun, their clothes drenched with sweat, the steel portion of their weapons hot to the touch.

Years of frustration were boiling over in the hearts and minds of the Sioux and Cheyenne warriors. This day would see leaders such as the famed Crazy Horse, Gall, Rain-In-The-Face, and others overwhelming and annihilating the elite Seventh Cavalry, and they would do so with a speed and determination that would make any West Point instructor proud.

As the troopers gave ground under pressure, some groups proved to be more orderly than others. However, when panic ensued, disintegration followed by death came very quickly.

After Lieutenant Calhoun's position was overrun, the remnants fled northward into Captain Keogh's Company I. But a mounted attack by Crazy Horse's warriors brought destruction on most of these as well. Soon all of the groups were killed, leaving only Custer's huddled mass to deal with.

The smoke and dust of battle, the screams of the wounded, and the sound of gunfire and eagle-bone whistles filled the air. As the fight continued to the spot known today as Last Stand Hill, the officers and men shot their horses, instantly transforming the animals into protective breastworks. The hostiles, firing various weapons and hurling arrows with metal heads[6] would engulf the boy-general and all those who looked to him for their deliverance. But today, there would be no deliverance, and an unlikely epitaph was about to be written.

When Custer fell, it was directly across from the camp of the Cheyennes, and what had been promised him as he sat under the Medicine Arrows had now come to pass. In this sense, his death became terribly ironic, and one the Cheyenne could take great pleasure in.

The spot where Custer fell is just short of the summit where the monument now stands. It is almost certain that Custer intended to reach this summit but was prevented from doing so. Perhaps reaching the top would have given Custer a little more time, but that time could be calculated in minutes only, and would have made absolutely no difference in his final outcome. Just as he would not help Reno, Reno could not help him.

When found, Custer was lying in a semi-propped up position between two other corpses. Witnesses said he looked very calm, which is not surprising. He had two bullet wounds, one in the left chest and one in the left temple, although this head wound was certainly a postmortem wound fired by a zealous Indian who just wanted to make sure that death was not being faked.

But how and when did the famous one die? There are in fact numerous accounts of George Armstrong Custer's death. The Indians were unaware at the time who it was they were killing, but once they discovered it was Long Hair whom they had defeated, it became fashionable to take credit for his death. In truth, it is impossible to determine who fired the shot that killed this military icon. Two months before his death, Rain-In-The-Face, who hated Captain Tom Custer because he had once had him arrested, made what I believe to be a fair assessment of the nature and ferocity of this battle when he said, "In that fight the excitement was so great that we scarcely recognized our nearest friends." [7]

One version of Custer's death, which appeared in the *New York Herald* in 1877, was a version given by Sitting Bull, who supposedly received the information from warriors returning from the fight. In it Custer, at battle's end, was only one of several troopers still alive, laughing and killing an Indian as he himself crumpled to the ground. To be sure, nothing would please white ears more than to think of their famous general dying in such a gallant manner. It certainly makes for good reading, but I believe that Sitting Bull's account of the death should be shelved within the fiction section, for I believe it contains little of what actually happened. Perhaps it was a well-intentioned attempt at topping off an otherwise disastrous affair—for the whites—with a happy ending.

One scenario which does at least seem plausible—but like the previous testimony, unprovable—is that Custer was shot by a young Oglala by the name of Joseph White Crow Bull as he journeyed down Medicine Tail Coulee. What gives this incident the ring of truth is that the man Joseph shot was not only wearing buckskin, as Custer was, but he was traveling beside a flag-bearing soldier, and most importantly, after being shot, a good many troopers were seen to close up around him.[8] If this report is indeed accurate, then Custer was at least felled, if not killed, early in the engagement. One can easily imagine the confusion which must have swirled in the minds of those who witnessed Custer, like a mere mortal, tumbling from his saddle. This was the unthinkable, the terrible reality come to life. Whether he made his way up the ridge to Last Stand Hill under his own power, or was borne up by his faithful subordinates, will forever remain within the realm of speculation, as so many other aspects of this quick and decisive battle. Yet if he were wounded at Medicine Tail Coulee, this could explain why so many officers died with Custer, instead of falling with their respective companies.

However death came to G.A.C., it is certain that he died as he had lived: a soldier. And I am convinced that as he saw the situation beginning to deteriorate before his eyes, he faced the situation with a calm resolve, determined to hold out to the end, and, true to his character, taking as many of his adversaries with him as possible.

On more than one occasion during the Civil War, Custer wrote to Libbie, telling her that even during the heat of battle, when shot and shell were screaming past his head, he was thinking of her.[9] Perhaps it was being so close to extinction that caused him to dwell with her mentally at such times. Whatever it was, when the heavens began to open before him, and he realized that all was lost, it probably was Libbie who burned in his mind in those final moments. He was paying the price that he had caused so many others to pay on so many other battlefields before, and he knew it. It is probable that as his consciousness began to fade away, it was Libbie that he was reaching out to one last time.

Unlike many of the troopers who fell that day, Custer was spared mutilation. However, according to the Cheyenne, Kate Big Head, two Cheyenne women recognized Custer and used sewing awls to puncture his ear drums so that in the afterlife he might hear better than he had while on earth. They were of course remembering the 1869 warning Custer received while sitting under the Medicine Arrows, and his promise never to make war with the Cheyenne people again.

The task of burying the dead fell to the survivors of Reno's hilltop siege. Because of the hard soil and shortage of shovels, most of the enlisted men were interrred under only a few inches of soil. Custer and the officers received a deeper and more thorough burial and also had rocks placed over their graves. All were buried at the places on the field where they had fallen. Within a year, the Army ordered that the officers' remains be disinterred and brought back East for formal burials by their families. The enlisted men were buried in a mass grave on Last Stand Hill.

What of Indian casualties? Estimates of Indian dead for the Custer battle run as high as one hundred and as low as forty. Whatever their true number, all had been removed from the field by the time General Terry reached the site on June 27. As was their custom, the Sioux left their dead in lodges or on scaffolds. The Cheyenne would place their dead within the sides of cliffs or in rock crevices. A trooper visiting the field in 1877 told of walking among the bones of the Sioux who had fallen through their scaffolds. In one of the skulls he spotted a bullet, fired no doubt from one of the dead men now occupying Custer hill. According to Chief Gall, the wounded of the battle fared little better than those killed instantly, with as many dying each day as were killed during the battle. Within the hearts and minds of both cultures, the valley of the Little Bighorn would never be the same.

Chapter Six

ALIVE, AND ON THE HILL

Before 1876 had ended, the first biography of Custer was published by Frederick Whittaker. It was clear from his work that he blamed Major Reno for Custer's demise, even demanding that the Army launch a full investigation. Reno, desperately wanting to clear his name, requested a court of inquiry be held in the matter. The Army quickly agreed, holding the hearing at the Palmer House in Chicago.

Beginning January 13, 1879, and continuing for four weeks, the Reno Court of Inquiry heard testimony from the survivors of Custer's command to determine if enough evidence existed to hold court martial proceedings against Reno. At one point during the examination, an interesting exchange occurred between Captain Myles Moylan and the court. From the questioning, it was clear that the court was interested in finding any degree of cowardice which could be linked to the command's departure from the timber.

Q: In regard to the command on top of the hill, wouldn't you sooner have been dejected on the top of the hill than dead in the timber?

A: Well, I would rather be dejected on the top of the hill than dead anywhere.

Obviously not satisfied with Moylan's answer, the self-righteous court recorder, Lieutenant Lee, later asked:

Q: Would it not have been better, as a soldier, to have been dead in the timber than dishonored on the hill?

A: I don't know that that is a proper question to put to me. Very few men but would prefer to die in the timber than to be on the hill degraded.

Degraded or not, as the Reno command re-formed atop the bluffs, there was a brief respite from the fighting as the hostiles focused on the annihilation of the five companies four miles to the north. The command, now rejoined, would spend the rest of the 25th and most of the 26th of June, fighting for their lives.

Soon after the Indians began leaving the Reno position, firing was heard erupting downstream. Some said they could hear volley firing while others said the firing was more general. If it was volley firing, then it was an attempt by Custer to draw attention to his plight. One can easily imagine him

Custer in 1863

(All photographs courtesy of Little Bighorn Battlefield National Monument)

Custer, as he appeared at Washita

Captain Thomas Custer

Captain F. W. Benteen

Major Marcus A. Reno

General Custer, wielding the pen under the watchful eyes of wife Elizabeth at Fort Abraham Lincoln.

Sitting Bull

Rain-In-The-Face

Low Dog
An excellent example
of Sioux determination.

barking out orders to fire, say, on the count of three. But the unified crack of the Springfield model 1873 carbines would go unanswered. In any event, whatever type of shooting was actually echoing throughout the valley, most thought that it involved Custer. Lieutenant Varnum remarked that, a few minutes after Benteen arrived on the hill, he too heard firing but that it sounded like "...a heavy fire—a sort of crash, crash..." adding that he thought Custer was having a "warm time" down there.[1] Even so, the idea that Custer's command was being wiped out never entered his mind, and Varnum was not alone in this belief. The idea that Custer could be wiped out was practically unthinkable.

Demoralization and the sense of being "whipped" certainly was a problem for a number of officers and enlisted men alike. Of course, no one likes to admit demoralization, especially military people, and so as time elapsed, certain individuals attempted to put a better face on the situation where possible. One of these was Lieutenant Hare, yet Lieutenant Godfrey remembers Hare meeting him atop Reno hill, shaking his hand and exclaiming "We've had a big fight in the valley, got whipped like hell and I am damned glad to see you." [2]

Upon reaching the top of the hill, Reno was seen blazing away with his pistol at Indians one thousand yards away. This must have been from utter frustration, as Reno was well aware that the pistol's effective range did not exceed one hundred yards. Benteen, who would later take great pains to avoid using the word "demoralized" when testifying before the Reno

Court of Inquiry, did admit years later in personal correspondence with an ex-Seventh Cavalry trooper just how bad a time certain officers were having. According to Benteen, his first sight upon reaching the hill was of Captain Moylan, who was "...blubbering like a whipped urchin, tears coursing down his cheeks." [3]

Using a carbine, but like Reno also out of range, Varnum was firing at the retreating hostiles. Some observers said he was crying as well. The flight from the valley had been an undeniably emotional one, whose cost in dead and wounded could have been greatly reduced had Reno exercised proper leadership, beginning with ordering the proper bugle calls while still in the timber.

Before the pack train had even arrived, Captain Thomas Wier took an unauthorized ride to a high point a little over one mile north of their present position. Benteen would later refer to Wier's northern ride as "a fit of bravado." [4] Soon Lieutenant Edgerly came galloping up with Troop D and a short time later was joined by other elements of the command, the idea being to open up communication with Custer. In the distance they could see a great deal of dust and activity in what turned out to be the Custer Battlefield. However, by this time the battle was well over, the only movements now occurring were the mutilating and the looting of the command.

But the Seventh's foray northward would be short-lived as the Sioux and Cheyenne, drunk with victory, came calling again on those occupying the hill.

The hilltop, which was destined to drink in a good deal of Seventh Cavalry blood, was described by Lieutenant Varnum as being "...rather rough. That is, the top was uneven and rolling..."[5] Being part of the famous Badlands, this uneven and rolling hilltop would in some ways prove to be more beneficial to the Indians as they fired from concealed positions, although the circular depression where Dr. Porter had his field hospital was quite effective in helping to shield the wounded and can easily be recognized today. Indeed, most of the land appears just as it did in the summer of 1876, with the exception of the Little Bighorn River whose snake-like course has changed somewhat over the years.

Charles Windolph said that the men had barely reached their positions back on the bluffs when the Indians, having surrounded them, began their attack.[6] Over the next three hours, Reno's command would suffer another eighteen men killed and forty-six wounded.[7] When the sun finally set on the hard-pressed command, Lieutenant Wallace remembered it going down as a "red ball."[8]

Although a number of the men feared a night attack by the hostiles, none would be forthcoming. Still, sleeping would be quite difficult for some. Lieutenant Edgerly passed Reno on several occasions during the night of the twenty-fifth. "He asked me what I had been doing," Edgerly remembered. "I said I had been asleep. He said 'Great God,' I don't see how you can sleep."

Between 2:30 a.m. and 3 a.m., as daylight began stretching itself across the command, it brought with it another onslaught from the Sioux and Cheyenne warriors. According to Lieutenant Wallace, between 10 a.m. and noon on the 26th, the fire was particularly heavy. Some Indians mistakenly set up firing positions outside the range of their guns, and the bullets from these weapons fell harmlessly among the soldiers who could then pick them up.[9] At times, the only targets the soldiers would have to aim at would be the puffs of smoke giving away the warriors' position. "There would be a lull..." Wallace remembered. "And then it would start again, and the bullets would come in like hail." [10] At times the troops would refuse to return fire, and after a while, the hostiles, feeling they had inflicted a good deal of damage, would rise from their cover and charge the soldiers, only to be repulsed by heavy fire. But even with this steady fussillade of .45-caliber bullets, some areas were more vulnerable than others, and as a result, certain companies suffered higher casualties. At times, some warriors came so close they were able to hurl dirt clods at the surprised troopers. One even managed to touch a dead soldier with a long stick.[11]

Because of this pressure, Benteen told Reno that unless something was done, the entire command could be overrun. Reno allowed Benteen to carry out his plans, and so, after assembling a group of men together, Benteen gave them a quick pep talk relating the problem and what he proposed to do about it. Leading the charge himself, Benteen drove the astonished Indians away, thereby eliminating a potentially disastrous problem. Although second in command on the hill, Benteen later testified, "Mind you, I was looking after things probably more than it was my business or duty to do." [12] Benteen was not alone in this sentiment. Lieutenant Godfrey found no comfort in Major Reno's indecision or lack of confidence. After discussing the situation with Captain Weir, Lieutenant Godfrey decided that it was "...Benteen we must look for the wisdom to deliver us." [13]

Although Benteen's Company H was exposed to a withering fire, their captain exhibited an absolute calm. "Captain Benteen came over and stood near where I was on a high point." Lieutenant Edgerly recalled, "The bullets were flying very fast there and I did not see why he was not riddled. He was perfectly calm; I remember there was a smile on his face." [14] Lieutenant Wallace also saw him in a very exposed position and wondered why he wasn't shot down. After warning him to take cover, he said Benteen responded "...something about the bullet not having been moulded yet to shoot him..." [15]

And while Reno failed to impress most people with his leadership while on the hill, it is quite clear that he at least kept his head during the siege. Yet more damning than his lack of action was his discussion with Benteen that the command should abandon the wounded and make their escape the night of the 25th—something Benteen would never agree to. "...I killed that proposition in the bud." [16] Benteen later related this incident to a former Seventh Cavalry trooper with whom he had been corresponding, yet he chose not to reveal it at the inquiry, the reasons of which remain a mystery today. Perhaps he felt that Reno had suffered enough. Far more likely, though, was his desire to protect the reputation of the regiment. In any case, official ears would never hear of this incident, and the character of the major would be the better for it.

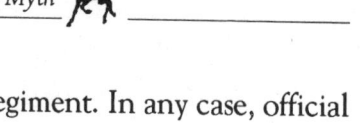

By late in the afternoon of the 26th, the great Indian camp began to depart, to the joy of the shattered troops they were leaving behind. Years later, certain Indians would make the absurd claim that the reason for their departure was that the soldiers had learned their lesson, and that there was no reason for further bloodshed. This again was the voice of the conquered Indian attempting to soothe white ears. In reality, Sioux scouts had seen the approach of the Terry-Gibbon column, and it wasn't white survival which concerned them but their own. It was time to head for safer ground.

As news of the disaster reached the white world, a sense of shock and disbelief began to engulf the nation. The closing of so many white eyes, including those of General Custer, caused the eyes of the living to open wide with amazement. After General Sherman received word in Philadelphia, a reporter pressed him for a response. "I don't believe it," he said "and I don't want to believe it if I can help it." [17] In Washington D.C., the War Department was kept busy as the families and friends of those in Indian country were seeking news of their fate.[18] From Salt Lake City came the report: "The citizens here are excited over the Custer massacre." and went on to offer their services should a "...regiment of frontiersman..." be needed. Twenty-four hours later, the people of Salt Lake City held a meeting and resolved to raise twelve hundred men over the next ten days to avenge the death of Custer and "...for the extermination of the Sioux Indians." [19]

Even former enemies came to the aid of the fallen military icon. Former Confederate General Joe O. Shelby, sent a telegram to President Ulysses S. Grant on July 7, which read "General Custer has been killed; we once fought him and now propose to avenge him. Should you determine to call volunteers, allow Missouri to raise one thousand." [20]

July 7th also saw a Senator Paddoc introduce a bill that would, if President Grant "...deems it necessary, to accept the services of volunteers from the state of Nebraska, and the territories of Wyoming, Colorado, Dakota, and Utah..." [21]

As might be expected, Monroe, Michigan, was devastated by the loss of its favorite son. By July 14, the townspeople, ever faithful to the general, took the first steps towards erecting a monument to honor the memory of the dashing young cavalryman.

But the loss to the Custer family was severe indeed. Killed with the General were his brother and close confidante in the Seventh, Captain Tom Custer. Their younger brother, Boston, who had been serving in the regiment as a forager, perished within feet of his famous brothers. The young "Autie" Reed, nephew of the general died, as did Lieutenant James Calhoun, brother-in-law to the Custer clan.

Despite the calls for revenge and annihilation, it would take another fourteen years before the final curtain would fall on the Sioux and Cheyenne at Wounded Knee in December, 1890. Like an unrelenting disease, the wheels of subjugation had been grinding away within this land for over four centuries. But Wounded Knee put an end to all that, and the possibility of Indian resistance was forever over. Not a pretty legacy, to be sure, yet it is often the only epitaph which can be written over those who break treaties and deal underhandedly with those in weaker positions than themselves. Of course, this mattered little to the victors. Their problem was finally over. And in time, the world would look away.

On the morning of July 8, people across the country were able to read the first official list of the dead and wounded. What follows is the headline from *The Bismarck Tribune Extra*.

Bismarck. July 8.—*The Bismarck Tribune Extra* gives the following official list of the killed and wounded in the recent encounter with the Indians on the Little Bighorn River.

Field, Staff, and Non-Commissioned Staff
G. A. Custer—Brevet Major General.
W. W. Cooke—Brevet Lieutenant.
Colonel Lord—Assistant Surgeon.
J. M. Dewolf—Acting Assistant Surgeon.
W. H. Sharrow— Sergeant Major.
Henry Vose—Chief Trumpeter.

Company A
Corporals Dollans and King; Privates Armstrong, Drinan, Moody, Rawlins, McDonald, Sullivan, and Switzer.

Company B
Lieutenant Hodgson; Privates Donovan and Moss.

Company C
Colonel T. W. Custer; Lieutenant H. M. Harrington; First Sergeant Bates; Sergeant Farley; Corporals French, Foley, and Ryan; Privates Allen, Brindle, King, Bucknall, Cissman, Engre, Brightfield, Fahold, Griffin, Hornet, Hattisdal, King, South, Lewis, Mayor, Phillips, Russell, Rex, Ranter, Short, Shea, Shode, Stuart, St. John, Shodied, Stanellan, Warren, Wyndam, and Wright.

Company D
Corporal Vincent Farrier; Privates Patrick Golden and Edward Hansen.

Company E
Captain A. E. Smith; Lieutenant Sturgis; First Sergeant Hohmeyer; Sergeants Egden and James; Corporal Hogan; and Privates Miller, Tweed, Noller, Cashan, Keifer, Andrews, Cresfield, Harrington, Hengge, Cavanaugh, Labaring, Mahoney, Schmidt, Lemon,

Sewanson, Riebold, O'Connell, Butler, Warren, Harrison, Gilbert, Ziller, Wash, Andrews, Assdelly, Burke, Cheever, McGue, McCarthy, Dogan, Maxwell, Scott, Babcock, Perkins, Tarbox, Dye, Tessier, Galvin, Graham, Hamilton, Snow, and Hughes.

Company K
First Sergeant Winney, Sergeant Hughes, Corporal Callahan, Trumpeter Helmer, and Private Ed. St. Clair.

Company I
Colonel M. Keogh; Lieutenant J. E. Porter; First Sergeant Varden; Sergeant Bastars; Corporals Wide and Morris Staples; Interpreters J. McGracer and J. Parden; Blacksmith H. Bailey; Trumpeters McElroy and Mooney; Privates Brondeharst, Barrey, Connor, Downing, Mason, Blarm, Mair, Baker, Boyle, Bath, Connor, Darcy, Davis, Farrell, Hilly, Haber, Hemil, Henderson, Leddison, O'Connor, Rood, Reese, Smith, Stellar, Stafford, Schoab, Smallwood, Tarr, Vanzant, Walker, Bryen, and Knight.

Company F
Colonel G. W. Yates; Lieutenant Bulley; First Sergeant Kenney; Sergeants Mersey, Vickary, and Wilkinson; Corporals Coleman and Freeman;

Farriers Braidy and Brandson; Blacksmith Fanning; Privates Atchison, Brown, Bruce, Brady, Burns, Sam. Colter, Carney, Donan, Donelly, Gardner, Hammond, Kleine, Kryarth, Human, Loose, Milton, Madison, Monroe, Ridden, Ometting, Sycfoz, Saunders, Warren, May, Levick, Kelly, Driscoll, Gillet, Gross, Holcomb, Hoen, Hittismer, Fred. Lehman, Lloyd, Macharge, Litchell, Lashally, O'Brien, Parker, Pitten, Post, Quinn, Reed, Rossburg, Tymons, Troy, Vanbramer, and Whalley.

Company G
Captain McIntosh; Sergeants Batziel and Colsedine; Corporals Martin, Hagman, and Wells; Farrier Henry Doge; Teamsters Crawford and Saddler; Privates Rogers, Monroe, McGinniss, Leballey, Stefferman, and Rupp.

Company H
Corporal Lee; Privates Jones and Meade.

Company M
Sergeant H. Harris; Corporals Sooltie and Struger; Privates Gorden, Klotzbursher, French, Myer, Smith, Semers, Tanner, Fenley, and Voight.

Twentieth Infantry
Lieutenant John J. Crittenden

Civilians
Boston Custer, Arthur Reed, Mark Kellogg, Charles Reynolds, and Frank C. Mann.

Indian Scouts
Bloody Knife, Bobtailed Bull, and Stab.

Recapitulation
Commissioned officers killed	14
Acting Assistant Surgeons	1
Enlisted men	237
Civilians	5
Indian scouts	3

The Wounded
The following is a full list of the wounded: Privates Davis Corry, Company I, Seventh Cavalry, right hip; Patrick McDonnell, Company D, left leg; Sergeant Kohn Wahl, Company H, back; Private Michael C. Mullen, Company K, right leg; Wm. George, Company H. left side, died July 3, at 4 a.m.; First Sergeant Wm. Heyn, Company A, left knee; Private John McVay, Company C, hip; Patrick Corcoran, Company K, right shoulder; Max Wicke, Company K, left foot; Alfred Whittier, Company C, right elbow; Peter Thompson, right hand; Jacob Diehl, Company A, face; J. H. Meyer, Company M, back; Roman Butler, Company M, right shoulder; Daniel Nevel, Company

M, left thigh; James Mullen, Company H, right thigh; Elijah Stroude, Company A, right leg; Sergeant Polk Carney, Company M, right hip; Private James E. Kennett, Company C, body, died July 5, at 3 o'clock; Francis W. Reeves, Company A, left hand and body; James Wibbur, Company M, left leg; Jasper Marshall, Company L, left foot; Sergeant James T. Riley, Company E, back and left leg; Private John T. Phillips, Company H, face and both hands; Sam. Swern, Company H, both thighs; Frank Brun, Company M, face and left thigh; Corporal Alex B. Bishop, Company H, right arm; Private James Foster, Company A, right arm; W. E. Harris, Company M, left breast; Charles H. Bishop, Company H, right arm; Fred. A. Olmstead, Company A, left wrist; Sergeant Charles White, Company A, right arm; Private Thomas P. Varney, Company M, right ear; Charles Campbell, Company G, right shoulder; John McGuire, Company C, right arm; Harry Black, Company H, right hand; Daniel McWilliams, Company H, right leg; Sergeant M. Riley, Company I, Seventeenth Infantry, left at Buford, constipation; Private David Atkinson, Company C, Seventh Cavalry, left off at Buford, constipation.

Conclusion

In any discussion concerning Custer's defeat at Little Bighorn, it is important first to acknowledge that the Indians won the battle because they did everything right. The response to the attack upon their village was swift and, like the wind, they pursued the soldiers without letup until all were killed or had been driven to the hill. Even so, without the direct help which they received from Custer, their victory would have been vastly different, and may not have occurred at all. Like the pieces to a puzzle, Custer's mistakes fit perfectly together with the decisions and movements of the Indians on that decisive day. Given these circumstances, the battle unfolded in the only way it could have. Still, certain scenarios could have evolved which might have turned the tide of battle in the Seventh's favor. In exploring these, we will not only see various roads, so to speak, which Custer could have taken, but we will be able to understand why this disaster became inevitable.

First of all, had the command remained a single fighting unit during the attack, it is highly unlikely that five companies would have been destroyed to a man, as they say. True, Custer may have been killed anyway and the Seventh Cavalry badly mauled, but the Indians would have suffered high casualties as well, and they would not have had the momentum that was gained by repulsing Reno without ever coming into contact with the forces under Benteen or McDougall. The isolated Custer, even with five companies, was easy to overwhelm. This would not have been the case had the entire regiment swept down into the valley completely intact. Had fate taken this direction, the Battle of Little Bighorn would have been a tremendous contest, and it is anyone's guess which side would have come out on top.

Second, had Reno continued his charge into the valley, he very well may have caused enough consternation within the camp to have aided Custer by making it possible for him to mount an attack southward toward Reno. Although this must have been Custer's plan, he forgot to inform Reno, who became seriously agitated by Custer's disappearance and failure to support him. Also, had Reno continued his attack, instead of making the detour into the woods and the subsequent gallop up the bluffs, he no doubt would have suffered higher casualties because he would have had to bear the brunt of the fighting until Custer could reach him. For Reno's men, this would have been disastrous. What would have occurred once Benteen arrived on the scene? No one will ever know.

The best scenario, of course, would have been the combined attack of the forces under Custer, Terry, and Gibbon. Had this occurred, the Indians would have most certainly suffered defeat. But as is always the case in war, anything can, and usually does happen. Regardless of the planning by the top brass, surprises always await those going into battle. For the U. S. Army, June had been a humiliating month, first with the defeat of General Crook on the 17th and then the Custer fiasco on the 25th. The Indians not only managed to win physically against the whites, but they triumphed over their enemies psychologically as well. Crook was so shaken by the ferocity of the Sioux attack along the Rosebud, that even with the prodding of General Sheridan, he refused to again move against the Indians until the second week of August.

Later on, Major Reno would be judged harshly by certain individual for his aborted charge in the valley. In some minds, Reno was the sole cause for the Custer defeat, but in light of the previously mentioned evidence, this charge is absurd. However, as commanding officer, it was his responsibility to bring order out of chaos, something he failed to do. As the highest ranking officer in the woods, it was his duty to see to it that the command fought its way out of the timber in an organized manner. First and foremost, he should have alerted the command to his plans to evacuate the woods by the use of bugle calls. Such an announcement would have been heard above the din of battle and would have been responded to. Had this occurred, the command could have exited the timber as one body, with the officers directing an organized fire that would have sent the Indians reeling back, forcing them to act in a defensive manner as well. Such an action would have saved many lives. I'm sure that during Reno's flight, the warriors could hardly believe their eyes as they sat on their ponies, pumping round after round from their Winchester rifles into the startled troopers. If blame is to be laid at Reno's feet for his conduct while in the valley, then it must be laid here. If Benteen's assertion that Reno wanted to abandon the wounded is true, then his greatest transgression occurred while on the hill—remaining hidden from the command. Although Reno would ask for and receive a court of inquiry, he would never be able emotionally to let go of that disastrous Sunday. Although officially exonerated by the court, he would never be free of those wanting to condemn him for his actions on that day. One of his harshest critiques was Libbie Custer herself, who felt that Reno was little more than a coward. Of course, in Libbie's mind, her dead general could do no wrong, and she would spend the rest of her life defending his actions and blaming others for her husband's defeat. This, of course, is the same type of closed-minded thinking which caused Custer to die in the first place. So much for lessons learned.

Captain Benteen, on the other hand, emerged from the debacle smelling like a rose, although some would blame him (Libbie among them) for not hurrying towards Custer once he received the fateful message from trumpeter Martini. But it was Custer who had sent Benteen on that useless gallop to the left. Having heard the dire warnings of the scouts, he felt that it was unwise to split the regiment and told Custer so. Besides, once Benteen arrived on the hill, he had his hands full reorganizing Reno's troops into a fighting unit again. Their attempt to help Custer, which was initiated by Captain Weir, was soon repulsed, and from that moment onward, it was a case of kill or be killed for those corralled on top of the spot known today as Reno Hill. After all, Custer could take care of himself. Of this, everyone was confident.

And while it is no secret that Benteen despised Custer, he was too much of a professional soldier to have knowingly abandoned him to his fate. His dislike of Custer was (in his mind) quite valid, going back many years. But Custer's failure to conduct a proper search for Major Elliott and his men during the Washita campaign, only intensified Benteen's hatred of him. This was not the soldierly thing to do and Benteen knew it.

At Little Bighorn, Benteen would conduct himself in the same cool-headed fashion that he always had. And the praise that he would receive from his fellow officers, and the enlisted men as well, for the leadership he displayed while on the hill is more than well deserved. Had Custer allowed Benteen to switch places with him on June 25, the outcome of the battle would have been very different.

In the final analysis, it appears that Custer, in his attempt to overwhelm the Sioux and Cheyenne, bit off a lot more than he could chew. In his mind, the Seventh Cavalry could not fail. Like Captain Fetterman, Custer possessed that arrogant belief that red warriors could never be a threat to white warriors regardless of their numbers. Between 1861 and 1865, Custer had overcome the best the South had to offer. Why should June 25, 1876, be any different? To be sure, Custer understood that death could be waiting for him during any battle. But his entire regiment being defeated by Plains Indians? Never! Such was the thinking of this thirty-six year-old commander of the Seventh U.S. Cavalry. And more than anything else, it would be this pattern of thinking that would cause the Indians to conquer him so easily. Caution had been thrown to the wind by Custer, and like the wind, the Seventh Cavalry was about to be carried away to the place in history it occupies today.

One factor which supposedly played a role in the fall of Custer was the jamming of the .45-caliber single-shot Springfield carbines which the troops carried. After walking the field over which Custer's men fell, Reno found a number of broken knife blades which were used by the frustrated troopers to extract the copper cartridges manually after the weapon failed to extract them properly. Evidently the problem was the cartridge rim, which had a tendency to snap off after the weapon became hot from firing, although a number of breakages were said to have occurred after only several rounds had been sent through the barrel. Reno's troops experienced some breakdowns while on the hill as well, but the problem overall seemed to be very small, so it is doubtful that weapon failure added significantly to Custer's demise. Be that as it may, it still must have been horrible for those few on

Custer Hill who did experience such jamming. Their terror can easily be imagined.

Recently, an unlikely testimony has come from the ground itself. After a grass fire swept over the battlefield in 1983, a thorough archaeological examination of the field was conducted. It proved to be very fruitful. Backed by a team of volunteers wielding that modern-day wonder, the metal detector, the archaeologists made some startling discoveries. First, they were able to locate numerous positions used by the Indians after finding the spent casings which came from their various weapons, as well as the soldiers' carbine bullets which impacted on those areas. Second, they were able to determine how various Indians traveled about the field during the fight, by identifying the unique pattern an individual weapon makes when the firing pin strikes the primer on the casing and certain marks which may appear as the casing is extracted.

But it wasn't just bullets and copper casings which littered the field. Tragic reminders of the fight came to light as well. A leg bone still inserted within the remains of an 1872 cavalry boot, the heel and sole of the boot almost completely intact. One of the most poignant finds was that of a wedding ring still encircling the finger bone of the long-dead husband.

When further excavations were being carried out at the Reno-Benteen position in May, 1989, a volunteer by the name of Monte Kloberdanz was destined to make one of the most significant discoveries in years. After growing weary of working and finding nothing in the prescribed digging area, he decided to venture down towards the Little Bighorn River.

As he was examining the area over which Reno's men crossed the river, he spotted something sticking out from the river bank. That something turned out to be a skull, minus the lower jaw bone, and two additional bones, which, after forensic studies were performed, turned out to be that of a white individual, approximately thirty to forty years old who died sometime in the 1870s. More precisely, June 25, 1876. The skull is once again beneath the earth, but this time its in the grounds of the National Cemetery at Little Bighorn Battlefield.

In December, 1991, Custer Battlefield National Monument underwent a name change. Proponents of the change said America has always named its battlefields after the name of the town or area in which the fighting occurred, which of course is true. A perfect example of this would be "Gettysburg," a town, and "Antietam," a creek. As can be expected, staunch defenders of keeping things the way they have always been, as well as those who are vocal defenders of Custer, decided this should never be. Even a descendant of Custer's threatened to haul his stuff out of the museum if the name change went through. But when I visited the site, now renamed Little Bighorn Battlefield National Monument on Memorial Day of 1992, they informed me that Custer's descendant had also passed away.

After resting one year upon the heights above the Little Bighorn River, Custer was returned to the place where his military career began, West Point. Although his death occurred only fifteen years after his graduation, Custer accomplished far more in that time than most of his peers achieved in much longer careers. When Custer's wife, Libbie, passed away in 1933, she was placed beside her husband whom she managed to outlive by more than half a century.

Acknowledgments

Whenever anyone undertakes to write about the important events of those who are now long dead, I believe it is very important to remember those who have gone before us, who diligently recorded the facts and circumstances which surrounded those lives. Without these individuals, much of what we call history would forever be lost to us and the researcher would virtually have nowhere to go. To the many fine people who contributed to recording the events surrounding the life of George Armstrong Custer, from field reporters to established authors, I thank you. To those among the living who aided me in my search, I am indebted to you in ways you cannot imagine, for in some cases we exchanged words without exchanging names.

I would like to thank specifically the folks at the Armor library at the Fort Knox military base near Radcliff, Kentucky, for their fine help and assistance. After all, they are the home of Cavalry and Armor! A big round of applause to the fine individuals in the research department at the Louisville Free

Public Library, especially those who were forced to retrieve a number of old, dust-covered government publications which hadn't been used in years. Special thanks must also go to Kitty Deernose, curator at Little Bighorn Battlefield National Monument, for her help with the photographs which are included in this book.

And finally, I would like to thank my family for all the support and patience they extended to me as I galloped after Custer as fast as he must have been galloping over those hot Montana hills so long ago. Without you I could not have finished the task.

NOTES

Chapter One
1. Frederick Whittaker, *A Complete Life of General Custer* (New York, 1876), p. 42.
2. Marguerite Merington, *The Custer Story: The Life and Intimate Letters of George Custer And His Wife Eizabeth* (New York, 1950), p.108.
3. Ibid, p. 66.
4. Ibid, p. 66
5. Ibid, p. 66
6. Ibid, p. 63.
7. Gregory J. W. Urwin, *Custer Victorious: The Civil War Battles of General George Armstrong Custer* (East Brunswick, N.J., 1983), p. 93
8. Ibid, p. 134.
9. David Neven, *The Soldiers* (New York, 1973), p. 188
10. Ibid, p.188.
11. Merington, *The Custer Story*, p. 105.
12. Frederic F. Van de Water, *Glory-hunter: A Life of General Custer* (Indianapolis, 1934), p.43.
13. Ibid, p. 43.

14. H. Norman Schwarzkopf, "CBS Reports: Schwarzkopf in Vietnam, A Soldier Returns."
15. *The Daily Louisville Commercial*, July 9, 1876.
16. Senate Executive Document, Number 33, 50th Congress, 1st session. Volume 1. Serial number 2504.
17. Senate Executive Document, Number 26. 39th Congress. Serial number 1277.

Chapter Two

1. Frances Paul Prucha, *The Great Father* (Norman, Oklahoma 1984), p. 65.
2. Ibid, p. 71.
3. Senate Executive Document, Number 26. 39th Congress. Serial number 1277.
4. George Armstrong Custer, *My Life On The Plains* (Norman, Okla., 1962), p. 314.
5. Ibid, p. 315.
6. Ibid, p. 318.
7. Ibid, p. 320.
8. Robert Utley, Ed. *Life In Custer's Cavalry: Diaries and Letters of Albert and Jennie Barnitz, 1867-1868* (New Haven, Connnecticut, 1977), p. 218.
9. Custer, *My Life On The Plains*, p. 331.
10. Utley, *Life In Custer's Cavalry*, p. 225.
11. Stan Hoig, *The Battle of The Washita* (Garden City, New York, 1976), p. 130-131.
12. Utley, *Life In Custer's Cavalry*, p. 226.
13. Custer, *My Life On The Plains*, p. 383.

14. General E. S. Godfrey, "Some Reminiscences, Including The Washita Battle," November 27, 1868. *The Cavalry Journal*, October, 1928. Number 153.
15. Ibid.
16. Ibid.
17. Ibid.
18. W. A. Graham, *The Custer Myth: A Source Book of Custeriana* (Harrisburg, Pa. 1953), p. 208.
19. Ibid, p. 208.
20. George Bird Grinnell, *The Fighting Cheyennes* (New York, 1955), p. 307.

Chapter Three

1. *The Courier Journal*, July 4, 1876.
2. Ibid.
3. Elizabeth Custer, *Boots and Saddles* (New York 1885), p. 207
4. Ibid, p. 218.
5. Ibid, p. 222.
6. The Official Record of The Reno Court Of Inquiry, F. F. Girard testimony (hereafter referred to as Reno Court).
7. Edward S. Godfrey, "Custer's Last Battle," *Century Magazine* January, 1892.
8. Ibid.
9. Ibid.
10. George C. Frison, *Prehistoric Hunters of the High Plains* (San Diego, Calif., 1978, 1991.), p. 197.
11. Girard testimony, Reno Court.

12. Edgar I. Stewart, *Custer's Luck* (Norman, Okla., 1955), pp. 259, 263.
13. Ibid, p. 258.
14. Godfrey, "Custer's Last Battle," *Century Magazine*.
15. Frazier Hunt, and Robert Hunt. *I Fought With Custer: The Story of Sergeant Windolph, Last Survivor of the Battle of the Little Bighorn* (New York, 1954), p. 74.

Chapter Four

1. Graham, *The Cavalry Journal*, July 1923
2. Stewart, *Custer's Luck*, p. 275.
3. Col. T. M. Coughlan, "The Battle of the Little Bighorn," *The Cavalry Journal*, No. 43, Jan.-Feb. 1934.
4. Graham, *The Custer Myth*, p. 179.
5. Graham, *The Cavalry Journal*, July, 1923.
6. Hunt and Hunt, *I Fought With Custer*, p. 76.
7. Benteen testimony, Reno Court.
8. Ibid.
9. Ibid.
10. Hunt and Hunt, *I Fought With Custer*, p. 78.
11. Girard testimony, Reno Court.
12. Benteen testimony, Reno Court.
13. Graham, *The Custer Myth*, p. 241.
14. Varnum Testimony, Reno Court.
15. Graham, *The Custer Myth*, p. 88.
16. Reno Court, p. 213
17. *St. Paul Pioneer Press*, July 18, 1886.
18. Moylan testimony, Reno Court.

19. Herendeen testimony, Reno Court.
20. Wallace testimony, Reno Court.
21. Ibid.
22. Moylan testimony, Reno Court.
23. Varnum testimony, Reno Court.
24. Doctor Porter's testimony, Reno Court.
25. Girard testimony, Reno Court.
26. Ibid,
27. Graham, *The Custer Myth*, p. 242.
28. Varnum testimony, Reno Court.
29. Thomas B. Marquis, *Wooden Leg: A Warrior Who Fought Custer* (Lincoln Neb., 1962), p. 221.
30. Reno testimony, Reno Court.
31. Porter testimony, Reno Court.
32. Herendeen testimony, Reno Court.

Chapter Five

1. Graham, *The Custer Myth*, p. 249.
2. Ibid.
3. Benteen testimony, Reno Court.
4. Ibid.
5. Richard A. Fox, *Archaeology, History, and Custer's Last Battle* (Norman, Okla., 1993), pp. 139, 243.
6. Ibid, p. 116
7. Evan S. Connell, *Son Of The Morning Star* (New York, 1984), p. 390.
8. Ibid, p. 413.
9. Merington, *The Custer Story*, pp. 98, 143.

Chapter Six

1. Varnum testimony, Reno Court.
2. Godfrey testimony, Reno Court.
3. Graham, *The Custer Myth*, p. 200.
4. Benteen testimony, Reno Court.
5. Varnum testimony, Reno Court.
6. Hunt and Hunt, *I Fought With Custer*, p. 101.
7. Stewart, *Custer's Luck*, p. 409.
8. Wallace testimony, Reno Court.
9. Heredeen testimony, Reno Court.
10. Wallace testimony, Reno Court.
11. Benteen testimony, Reno Court.
12. Ibid.
13. Godfrey, "Custer's Last Battle," *Century Magazine*, January 1892.
14. Edgerly testimony, Reno Court.
15. Wallace testimony, Reno Court.
16. Graham, *The Custer* Myth, p. 192.
17. *The Courier Journal*, July 7, 1876.
18. Ibid.
19. Ibid.
20. *The Daily Louisville Commercial*, July 8, 1876.
21. Ibid.

Bibliography

Ambrose, Stephen E. *Crazy Horse and Custer*. Garden City, New York, 1975.

Brady, Cyrus Townsend. *Indian Fights and Fighters*. Lincoln, Neb., 1971.

Brininstool, E. A. *Troopers With Custer*. New York, 1952.

Brown, Dee. *Fort Phil Kearny: An American Saga*. New York, 1962.

Connell, Evan S. *Son Of The Morning Star*. New York, 1984.

Custer, Elizabeth. *Boots and Saddles*. New York, 1885.

Custer, George Armstrong. *My Life On The Plains*. Norman, Okla., 1876, 1962.

Fox, Richard A. *Archaeology, History, and Custer's Last Battle*. Norman, Okla., 1993.

Frison, George C. *Prehistoric Hunters of the High Plains*. San Diego, Calif., 1978, 1991.

Godfrey, Edward S. "Custer's Last Battle." *Century Magazine*, January 1892.

——— *The Cavalry Journal*. Vol. 37, No.153. October, 1928.

Graham, W. A. *The Custer Myth: A Source Book of Custeriana*. New York, 1953.

Grinnell, George Bird. *The Fighting Cheyennes*. New York, 1915.

Hofling, Charles K. *Custer and the Little Bighorn: A Psychobiographical Inquiry*. Detroit, Mich., 1981.

Hoig, Stan. *The Sand Creek Massacre*. Norman, Okla., 1961.

——— *The Battle of the Washita*. Garden City, New York, 1976.

Hunt, Frazier and Robert Hunt. *I Fought With Custer: The Story of Sergeant Windolph*. New York, 1947.

Kiem, Deb Randolph. *Sheridan's Troopers on the Border*. Philadelphia, Pa., 1891.

Marquis, Thomas B. *Wooden Leg: A Warrior Who Fought Custer*. Lincoln, Neb., 1962.

Merington, Marguerite. *The Custer Story: The Life and Intimate Letters of General George A. Custer and His Wife Elizabeth*. New York, 1950.

Miller, David Humphreys. *Custer's Fall*. New York, 1957.

Nevin, David. *The Old West: The Soldiers*. New York, 1973.

Stewart, Edgar I. *Custer's Luck*. Norman, Okla., 1955.

Urwin, Gregory J. W. *Custer Victorious: The Civil War Battles of General George Armstrong Custer*. East Brunswick, N.J., 1983.

Utley, Robert M. ed. *Life In Custer's Cavalry: Diaries and Letters of Albert and Jennie Barnitz. 1867-1868*.

—— *Cavalier In Buckskin*. Norman, Okla., 1988.

Van de Water, Frederic F. *Glory-Hunter: A Life of General Custer*. New York, 1934.

Whittaker, Frederick. *A Complete Life Of General George A. Custer*. New York, 1876.

Newspapers

The Daily Louisville Commercial

St. Paul Pioneer Press

The Courier Journal

The Chicago Times

The New York Herald

The record of the Reno Court of Inquiry, published daily by *The Chicago Times*, 1879.

About the Author

Kevin M. Sullivan was born forty years ago in Louisville, Kentucky, where he lives today with his wife Linda, and daughter Sarah. His interest in military conflicts goes back to the time when he first saw the Japanese flag that his father brought home from World War II. In 1972, and again in 1974, he had the opportunity of touring the battlefields of western Europe pertaining to the First and Second World Wars, where he conducted interviews with some former combatants and eyewitnesses to the conflicts. *Shattering The Myth* is his first book.